Adults Just Wanna Have Fun

ALA Editions purchases fund advocacy, awareness, and accreditation programs for library professionals worldwide.

adults just wanna have fun

AUDREY BARBAKOFF

programs for emerging adults

ala
editions

An imprint of the American Library Association

CHICAGO   2016

© 2016 by the American Library Association

Extensive effort has gone into ensuring the reliability of the information in this book; however, the publisher makes no warranty, express or implied, with respect to the material contained herein.

ISBN: 978-0-8389-1391-8 (paper)

Library of Congress Cataloging-in-Publication Data

Names: Barbakoff, Audrey, author.
Title: Adults just wanna have fun : programs for emerging adults / Audrey Barbakoff.
Description: Chicago : ALA Editions, an imprint of the American Library Association, 2016. |
    Includes bibliographical references and index.
Identifiers: LCCN 2015033081 | ISBN 978-0-8389-1391-8
Subjects: LCSH: Libraries—Activity programs—United States.
Classification: LCC Z716.33 .B37 2016 | DDC 025.5—dc23 LC record available at http://lccn.loc.gov/2015033081

Cover design by Kimberly Thornton. Images © Shutterstock, Inc.
Text design by Alejandra Diaz in the Freight Text Pro and Colaborate typefaces.

♾ This paper meets the requirements of ANSI/NISO Z39.48–1992 (Permanence of Paper).
Printed in the United States of America

20   19   18   17   16   5   4   3   2   1

CONTENTS

Select handouts from this book
are available at **alaeditions.org/webextras**.

ACKNOWLEDGMENTS

I WOULD LIKE to thank the many people who generously shared their time, expertise, and ideas to bring this book to life. To the fantastic librarians who enthusiastically shared their programs with me—Christy Estrovitz, Andrew Fuerste-Henry, Tracy Gossage, Sarah Jaffa, Amy Mather, Trent Miller, John Pappas, Sarah Smith, Leah White, and Jessica Zaker—I remain in awe of your brilliance and creativity. Sharing these success stories would not be possible without the dedication and support of my editor, Jamie Santoro, and the ALA Editions team.

My deep gratitude goes to Amanda Moss Struckmeyer, Manya Shorr, Rebecca Judd, and Jill Jean for their mentorship and encouragement. And to my life support system, my husband Brett and rescue dog Hermione, thank you for your endless patience and support.

PREFACE

LOOK AROUND THE public library. Who do you see?

Perhaps a few senior citizens read books and newspapers in one corner, while others check their e-mail at the public computers. Young children and their parents head toward the storytime room. A group of teenagers, which seems to be larger every year, studies and relaxes in the teen space.

One age demographic is notably missing: adults in their twenties and thirties. The millennial generation is the largest in history, outnumbering even its baby boomer parents. So why are there so few in the library?

Simply, librarians are failing to serve this group. Emerging adults have unique needs, different from both teens and older adults, and different from the needs of adults of the same age in earlier generations.

This book contains practical, actionable instructions for creating programs that will attract and retain emerging adult library patrons. By recognizing the importance of play and fun for adults, these programs can help public librarians build adult audiences that are as engaged and inspired as our youth.

Because libraries have only begun to recognize the need to serve emerging adults as a distinct group, a programming librarian may face extra obstacles in reaching them. How will she get funding and support for her events? How will he design and promote an effective program for a new audience? This chapter will serve to address the most pressing aspects of those questions.

Who Are Emerging Adults?

In order to program successfully for emerging adults, we must understand who they are and what they need. As expenses rise, wages stagnate, and the importance and length of higher education increases, modern adulthood is changing.

Due to a combination of financial and social factors, Americans now hit the classic milestones of adulthood (marriage, homeownership, parenthood) later, if at all. The days of turning eighteen, settling down with a good steady job, and starting a family are long over. Instead, a uniquely lengthy period of transition from adolescence to traditional adulthood has emerged.

Researchers believe this extended phase has given rise to an entirely new developmental period, which they call emerging adulthood.[1] Though the concept is relatively new, its exact meaning is already expanding. When psychology professor Jeffrey Arnett coined the term in 2000, it referred to adults ages eighteen to twenty-five.[2] His 2013 book on the subject included adults up to age twenty-nine.[3] As Gallup and Pew each separately studied the percentage of younger adults still living with their parents, often considered a hallmark for the expanded transitional period of emerging adulthood, both included adults through age thirty-four.[4]

Ultimately, though, these age brackets are in flux because they are merely general estimates of when a person is likely to go through certain experiences. Research suggests that five main characteristics define emerging adulthood: identity exploration, instability, self-focus, feeling in-between, and a sense of possibility and optimism.[5] Exploring these features is a very individual process that can take place at many points along the age spectrum of younger adults. Perhaps because of this, researchers of emerging adults choose different age ranges for their data, making it impossible to consistently compare a narrow range of ages. Therefore, for the purposes of this book emerging adulthood will be defined broadly as people in their twenties and early thirties, usually without children.

The reading and library use habits of emerging adults indicate that they have the potential to become a core part of our user base. According to a Pew Internet study, Younger Americans and Public Libraries, emerging adults are avid readers.[6] Eighty-eight percent of Americans under thirty report reading a book in the last year, compared to 79 percent of those older than thirty. This age group loves to read and learn, making them a perfect match for library services.

However, this is also a population we risk losing as library users for life. Emerging adults consistently rank libraries as less important than older groups do. Only 19 percent of people under thirty say that the library closing would have a major impact on them, compared to 32 percent of those over thirty. Fifty-one percent think it would have a major impact on their community, as opposed to 67 percent of older people. With this loss of value, the erosion of library usage among younger adults can happen swiftly. In November 2012, 56 percent of adults eighteen to twenty-four had visited a library that year; just one year later, that figure had dropped to 46 percent.[7]

Despite some worrisome trends, many emerging adults currently use and feel positively about the library. If we apply our resources to reaching emerging adults, we can engage these readers and learners at an often-overlooked moment in their lives.

Why Make the Effort?

Serving emerging adults is an incredible opportunity to create lifelong library lovers. People attach special emphasis to things that happen to them at this point in their lives. The "events of emerging adulthood are most often recalled as the most important" life moments, writes Jennifer Lynn Tanner.[8] During these years people are consolidating their sense of self, forming a stable adult personality based on the choices they make. As such, "the choices and decisions made during this era . . . define personal biographies across the life span."[9] If librarians can instill a passion for the library during those years, perhaps we could create truly lifelong users.

While emerging adulthood is creating new opportunities for public libraries, it also highlights our failure to recognize some existing ones. Historically, libraries have attracted users at key turning points in their lives. For adults, this has often meant parenthood and retirement. Librarians have long counted on affordable access to children's books, enriching entertainment for families, and relationships with other parents to bring disconnected younger adults back to the library when they become parents. However, as emerging adulthood is characterized by the delay of milestones like having children, serving young children is no longer a reliable way to attract adults in their twenties and thirties to the library.

When we try to consider the needs of adults in this age group, we reveal a stark absence in public library programs. We have never consistently offered programs to appeal to these adults themselves. Even when people in their twenties and thirties come to the library as parents, we provide little or nothing to appeal to their own personal interests beyond their children. Even if everyone had large families and flocked to the library for youth programs, even if currently childless emerging adults start families later in life and become avid users for their children, we would still be failing to serve them adequately as individuals. Why not create programs for these adults so that they continue to love libraries for themselves, independent of their family choices?

By reaching emerging adults, librarians can instill a passion for libraries that does not depend solely on milestones. Currently, the design of library programs may encourage intermittent use throughout life—during childhood, as a parent, as a retiree. If libraries can prove relevant, meaningful, and joyful for emerging adults, we may be able to create true lifelong engagement without gaps.

How Do I Program for Emerging Adults?

Emerging adults, by and large, do not think to look to the library for programs. More than a third of adults under thirty say they know little or nothing about what their local library has to offer them—no surprise, since the answer has historically been "not much."[10] To attract this new audience, fun and play are indispensable. A splashy, unique, high-interest program at a convenient time and place, advertised well to a specific target audience, has the power to change minds. Yet it is not necessary, or even desirable, to completely abandon the library's educational mission to do this. The most successful adult programs will combine learning and play for a powerful, engaging experience that is unique in your community.

When you read the last paragraph, was your knee-jerk reaction that "learning" or "education" would never attract young adults looking for fun experiences? Did these words conjure up devastatingly boring images of lectures and PowerPoint slides? Librarians, administrators, and patrons alike absorb this perception from pop culture depictions all around us. We have internalized the idea that adult learning looks silent, serious, passive, and difficult.

In the immortal words of the Jedi master, it is time to unlearn what we have learned . . . about learning.

The very best learning happens through fun. It happens through play. Active participation, excitement, and joy are not fluff. They are not frivolous. They are not extras to be valued and funded only after the "real" or "serious" educational programs have been accomplished. "Play is a catalyst for learning," writes Scott Nicholson, professor of Game Design and Development and director of the Brantford Game Network and the BGNLAB at Wilfrid Laurier University in Brantford, Ontario, "as learning happens best when players are encouraged to explore and choose a path that is meaningful to their backgrounds and interests."[11]

Numerous studies bear out the critical importance of adult play. Undergraduates in science, technology, engineering, and math courses are 55 percent more likely to fail a lecture-based class than one with even a little active learning. Active learning also increases average test scores by more than half a letter grade. "We've got to stop killing student performance and interest . . . by lecturing," that study's lead author, Scott Freeman, concluded.[12] The majority of these undergraduates are likely between eighteen and thirty, the very target population for the programs in this book. If lectures and passive learning don't engage them in the classroom, they certainly will not seek out similar experiences in the library. Active and participatory learning is essential, fundamental, and indispensable to engaging and educating emerging adults.

Further studies reveal that play is as important in real-world settings as it is inside the classroom. It builds the skills that are most crucial to today's flexible, fast-paced, global workplaces. "Play promotes problem solving and creativity," write the authors of *Einstein Never Used Flashcards: How Our Children REALLY Learn—and Why They Need to Play More and Memorize Less*.[13] They cite an experiment in which children were allowed to play with a coveted toy, but only if they were able to retrieve it from a far-away box without standing up. As tools, the children had several toy sticks that could be put together. Some children had unstructured play with the sticks beforehand, others were simply shown the answer by the researcher, and a third group received no guidance at all.

The average adult learner (or librarian, or administrator!) might guess that the children who were shown the solution had the best results, but this was not the case. Although some of these children imitated the correct procedure immediately, many were unable to do so on the first try. These children simply gave up. They may have felt that they were incapable, that they had failed to learn from the researcher and therefore could not learn how to do it.

The children who played, however, worked out their solutions through trial and error. When one tactic failed, they tried something else. They persevered until they achieved their goal. This group of learners developed creativity and resilience.

Though this study was with children, we can extrapolate its themes to adulthood; playful learning is not only more enjoyable, it is more effective. It all boils down to one simple equation, conclude the authors: "PLAY = LEARNING."[14] Through play, the library can encourage the flexible education that adults need in the modern workforce, developing skills like creativity, critical thinking, and resilience.

Emerging adults crave this kind of fulfilling, fun educational opportunity. Demand for adult summer camps, preschools, and coloring books has exploded.[15] A 2013 Pew study found that 53 percent of people ages sixteen to twenty-nine said the library "definitely should" offer more interactive learning experiences, with an additional 37 percent saying they "maybe should."[16] With more than 90 percent of emerging adults expressing some interest in hands-on interactive learning at the library, playful programs have the potential to be as popular as they are meaningful.

The programs in this book create a space for younger adults to be playful, exploratory, hands-on, messy, and loud. They are fun—and that is exactly what makes them so valuable.

How Do Adults Play?

In our culture, play and childhood have become nearly synonymous. "Most of us consider play to be left over from recess," says play expert Fred Donaldson. "We put away play when we put away childish things."[17] Studies support the conclusion that as we age, we learn to consider ourselves less creative, less imaginative, less playful. In 1968, researchers administered a creativity test to 1,600 five-year-olds. Nearly all—98 percent—scored "highly creative." Five years later, only 30 percent of the same children ranked "highly creative," and by age fifteen, only 12 percent did. The same test, administered to more than a quarter million adults in subsequent years, showed only 2 percent as highly creative.[18]

Think about that: 98 percent of children, but only 2 percent of adults, are highly creative. When do we lose our ability to imagine, to explore? Is this an inevitable result of growing up? Not at all, the researchers determined. "What we have concluded," wrote project lead George Land, "is that noncreative behavior is learned."[19]

Noncreative behavior is learned. If adults learned to stop playing somewhere along the line, then we can learn to play again. "Adults actually have a lot of potential," says Alan Gregerman, author of *Lessons from the Sandbox* and proponent of a "Take your Adult to the Playground" Day.[20] But what educational institution can help adults relearn exploration, enthusiasm, and creative failure? Who can give adults a safe place to be silly and vulnerable, without worrying about maintaining a perfect image or attaining a degree-worthy skill set? Of course, this is the perfect job for the public library.

So what programs can librarians provide to rekindle the spark? How do adults relearn how to play?

Since creating playful programs for adults is new to many libraries, we need to examine what play really is and how it works. Fortunately, librarians do not need to just hold our collective breath and hope our programs will somehow be fun. In light of the convincing evidence that adult play is a powerful force for learning, it has become a serious focus for research and scholarship.

One of the most prominent scholars on play and games in libraries is Scott Nicholson, professor of Game Design and Development at Wilfrid Laurier University in Ontario. Nicholson identifies six key components of meaningful play, which he has dubbed its RECIPE:[21]

- **Reflection**—assisting participants in finding other interests and past experiences that can deepen engagement and learning
- **Engagement**—encouraging participants to discover and learn from others interested in the real-world setting
- **Choice**—developing systems that put the power in the hands of the participants
- **Information**—using game design and gameplay concepts to allow participants to learn more about the real-world context
- **Play**—facilitating the freedom to explore and fail within boundaries
- **Exposition**—creating stories for participants that are integrated with the real-world setting and allowing them to create their own.

Not all of these elements will apply to any given program, but considering which ones are at work, and how, can help librarians encourage playfulness. For example, a program on making homemade spa products gives people information about how to reduce chemical exposure and save money, creates engagement as they share ideas and opinions with other participants, provides choice about what colors and scents to use, and lets them play as they invent and experiment with various combinations.

Thinking about these elements can also help us target areas for improvement in our existing programs. For example, we could increase choice in the spa products program by offering a wider variety of scents and colors. We could introduce an element of reflection by asking people to discuss their motivations for participating or to share their results.

Most play and gaming research is not directly focused on libraries, but it can still impact how we consider play in our programs. These studies often examine how elements of games and gaming affect our brains to create a sense of fun and play. They may explore applications of those features to encourage greater engagement with real-world issues.

Much of this recent research on adult play has focused on games and gamification, a subsection of the broader subject of play. Gamification means applying a gameful layer to a non-game, real-life activity.[22] The most familiar library example would be summer reading programs. This research focus on games and gaming is understandable. Because games have end points and goals that can result in quantifiable real-world impacts, they lend themselves neatly to study and have direct, profitable applications in business and marketing. Prominent games and gaming researchers include Jane McGonigal, Ian Bogost, and Adam L. Penenberg.

However, other types of research are also needed for designing playful emerging adult programs. Despite significant overlap, play is not exactly the same as a game. Games are a type of play, but not all play is gaming. "A game is, at its root, a structured experience with clear goals, rules that force a player to overcome challenges, and instant feedback."[23] Free, imaginative play can lack some or all of these structural elements.

Play activities are defined as being done by choice rather than obligation, for fun, in a spirit of creativity and exploration. The mechanics of a game may be applied, or not. Though this book will include games and gameful programs, many high-engagement, low-cost library events engage adults through exploratory or imaginative play alone.

Recent non-gameplay research on adults is limited. The bulk of general play studies are still conducted with children; even those concerned with adult creativity and success often focus on the role of childhood.[24] Researchers who do examine playfulness in adults often eschew that word in favor of language with direct appeal to the financial interests of businesses—think innovation, disruption, creativity, and problem solving. While all this research is highly valuable and can inform librarians' program choices, it does not illuminate the full spectrum of play in adult life. For a fuller picture, it is hoped the focus of this field of research will expand to include adult play of all kinds. For now, the result is a still-evolving picture of what adult play can be in libraries.

So what is a programming librarian to do, if the answers we want are not forthcoming? Of course, we will find them by playing! Programming librarians can experiment—can play—in order to discover what delights adults in our communities. Try programs that sound exciting and engaging. Fail. Tinker. Try again. And all throughout, make it fun, make it messy, make it joyful.

Look to Youth Services

Luckily, the adult services librarian trying to design programs for playful learning is not alone. You might just have an expert in this subject sitting next to you. Children's librarians have made the intersection of play and education a standard pillar of youth library service for years. The federal Institute of Museum and Library Services states matter-of-factly that young people "learn best . . . [through] content-rich, play-based experiences."[25] Research abounds on the importance of play in children's learning. The National Association for the Education of Young Children devotes an entire section of its website (www.naeyc .org/play) to research and information on this topic.

Children's programs at libraries reflect this understanding. Consulting a storytime handbook, such as *I'm a Little Teapot!: Presenting Preschool Storytime* by Jane Cobb, reveals dozens of pages of programs which include not only read-aloud books but fingerplays, songs, movement, and crafts. The first public library summer reading games appeared in 1890, and 95 percent of public libraries now provide them.[26] The New York Public Library youth calendar for summer 2014 includes fun, experiential programs like building robots, meeting live animals, making squirt gun volcanoes, attending parties, playing video games and chess, and learning Chinese Ribbon Dancing, just to name a few.[27]

With this variety of playful youth events, and this solid understanding and wide acceptance of their importance, it is hardly surprising that 70 percent of people attending library programs are there for children's activities. However, adults are hungry for library programs that will offer the same benefits to them. Overall library program attendance for all ages increased almost 25 percent between 2004 and 2011, according to the most recent data currently available.[28] Play is a powerful force for education at all ages. After all, to misquote Dr. Seuss, a person's a person, no matter how large.

Build on the success of children's librarians and enlist them as partners and guides. Many reference librarians can tell stories about adults coming to the desk, asking half-jokingly if they can attend a children's or teen program. That is a perfect moment to try aging up that program for adults! Youth librarians can share the research that guides them, the words of persuasion that won the library board's support for an innovative program, and the programming ideas that keep their events fun and engaging.

Youth librarians are also experts in advocating for the importance of play. They arrange fun, playful programming on a regular basis, and usually receive funding and broad support for it. Even as adult services librarians struggle to articulate the value of gaming events, sci-fi parties, and maker programs to our Friends, foundation, and boards, youth librarians are lauded for understanding and maximizing the role of play in learning. In addition to borrowing ideas for programs and events from our youth-focused counterparts, adult services librarians can learn to use their successful language and framing.

By working in partnership with children's and teen librarians, adult services librarians can make a clear case for programming that supports a pattern of playful exploration that begins in infancy and lasts a lifetime.

How Do I Convince My Funders?

The language librarians use to talk about fun emerging adult programming is as essential as the programs themselves. As long as these classes and events are seen as extraneous fluff, they will struggle for funding and support. The adult services librarian may know all about the importance and power of play in education, especially when reaching out to this chronically underserved age group, but her projects will never get off the ground without the backing of the library director, the branch manager, colleagues, Friends and Foundation groups, and the community at large.

Winning this support is easier than you may think. We can often revolutionize people's perspective on these programs simply by changing a few words. This is the key: use language that draws a clear connection to the library's fundamental values.

"What is valued gets funded," states Valerie Gross, CEO of the Howard County (Md.) Library. [29] Gross is an astonishing success story about the power of words. By changing *only* the language her library system used to describe itself, she was able to significantly increase the library's perceived value in the community. She realized that her community and local government valued education highly, and so she aligned the library's language with an explicit educational mission. Without making a single change to the events themselves, storytime became children's classes. Outreach became community education. Programs became classes, seminars, workshops, and events. [30] "[P]ut yourself in the shoes of your county executive (or mayor, governor, or a taxpayer voting on a tax increase)," she proposes, "then ask yourself which you would fund more generously—or cut less—*storytime* or *children's classes that teach the foundations of reading*?"

Consider the values of the library where you will propose an emerging adults program. Across systems, research has identified "literacy and learning" as a cornerstone of the library's value. "What is the value of libraries? Through lifelong learning, libraries can and do change lives, a point that cannot be overstated."[31] Adult services librarians need to take a look at their library's mission, vision, and values statements. Chances are good that concepts like "lifelong learning" and "education" will feature prominently. Therefore, it is crucial to frame proposals for emerging adult programs in the context of education.

This language makes it clear that your events are an essential piece of the library's mission and a key component of its value. When seen in that light, funding, supporting, and caring about emerging adult programs becomes common sense.

Using This Book

As I have played with programs for emerging adults, I have found three overarching categories that consistently engage twentysomethings and thirtysomethings with fun and play. This book is designed around those themes. They are: Get Dirty, Get Out, and Get Together. Each type of activity is a shortcut through the research and practice described here and throughout the book. They are practical suggestions you can immediately apply to create playful environments for your patrons.

These categories, and the programs in them, are a jumping-off point for you to play. The events have been tested in the real world and were considered successful by the librarians who designed them. We experimented, tried, failed, and tried again until we landed on the programs that worked for us. Now you can do the same. Let's go play!

NOTES

1. J. J. Arnett and Jennifer Lynn Tanner, *Emerging Adults in America: Coming of Age in the 21st Century* (Washington, DC: American Psychological Association, 2006).
2. J. J. Arnett, "Emerging Adulthood: A Theory of Development from the Late Teens through the Twenties," *American Psychologist* 55 (2000): 469–480.
3. J. J. Arnett and Elizabeth Fishel, *When Will My Grown-Up Kid Grow Up? Loving and Understanding Your Emerging Adult* (New York: Workman Publishing, 2013).

4. Jeffrey M. Jones, In U.S., 14% of Those Aged 24 to 34 Are Living with Parents, www.gallup.com/poll/167426/aged-living-parents.aspx; Richard Fry and Jeffrey S. Passel, In Post-Recession Era, Young Adults Drive Continuing Rise in Multi-Generational Living, July 17, 2014, www.pewsocialtrends.org/2014/07/17/in-post-recession-era-young-adults-drive-continuing-rise-in-multi-generational-living/.

5. J. J. Arnett and Elizabeth Fishel, *When Will My Grown-Up Kid Grow Up? Loving and Understanding Your Emerging Adult* (New York: Workman Publishing, 2013).

6. Kathryn Zickuhr and Lee Rainie, Younger Americans and Public Libraries: How Those Under 30 Engage with Libraries and Think about Libraries' Role in Their Lives and Communities (Washington, DC: Pew Research Center, September 10, 2014), www.pewinternet.org/files/2014/09/PI_Younger AmericansandLibraries_091014.pdf.

7. Ibid.

8. Jennifer Lynn Tanner, "Recentering During Emerging Adulthood: A Critical Turning Point in Life Span Human Development," In *Emerging Adulthood: A Theory of Development from the Late Teens through the Twenties*, J. J. Arnett, ed. (Washington, DC: American Psychological Association, 2006).

9. Ibid.

10. Kathryn Zickuhr and Lee Rainie, Younger Americans and Public Libraries: How Those Under 30 Engage with Libraries and Think about Libraries' Role in Their Lives and Communities (Washington, DC: Pew Research Center, September 10, 2014), www.pewinternet.org/files/2014/09/PI_Younger AmericansandLibraries_091014.pdf.

11. Scott Nicholson, "Strategies for Meaningful Gamification: Concepts behind Transformative Play and Participatory Museums," presented at *Meaningful Play* (Lansing, MI: 2012), http://scottnicholson.com/pubs/meaningful strategies.pdf.

12. National Science Foundation, Enough with the Lecturing, 2014, http://nsf.gov/news/news_summ.jsp?cntn_id=131403&org=NSF&from=news.

13. Kathy Hirsh-Pasek, Roberta M. Golinkoff, and Diane E. Eyer, *Einstein Never Used Flash Cards: How Our Children REALLY Learn—and Why They Need to Play More and Memorize Less* (Emmaus, PA: Rodale, 2003).

14. Ibid.

15. Adrienne Raphel, "Why Adults Are Buying Coloring Books (for Themselves)," *The New Yorker* (July 12, 2015), www.newyorker.com/business/currency/why-adults-are-buying-coloring-books-for-themselves.

16. Kathryn Zickuhr, et al., Younger Americans' Library Habits and Expectations (Washington, DC: Pew Internet, 2013), http://libraries.pewinternetorg/2013/06/25/younger-americans-library-services/.

17. Rick Ansorge, "All Work and No Play Puts Adults Out of Touch: Playfulness Can Be Key to Creativity," *Colorado Springs Gazette—Telegraph* (December 21, 1990): D1.

18. Susan Vaughn, "Zen at Work; To Think Outside Box, Get Back Into Sandbox; Now That Creativity Can Mean Corporate Survival, Employees Have to Learn How to Make Work into Child's Play," *Los Angeles Times* (January 11, 1999): 3.

19. Ibid.

20. Don Idenburg, "Learning from the Minds of Babes; Book Brings Sandbox Creativity to Workplace," *The Washington Post* (September 14, 2000): C.4.

21. Scott Nicholson, "A RECIPE for Meaningful Gamification," in *Gamification in Education and Business*, Wood, L. and Reiners, T., eds. (Switzerland: Springer, 2015), http://scottnicholson.com/pubs/recipepreprint.pdf.

22. Adam L. Penenberg, *Play at Work: How Games Inspire Breakthrough Thinking* (New York: Portfolio Hardcover, 2013).

23. Ibid.

24. Recent examples include *Pretend Play in Childhood: Foundation of Adult Creativity* by Sandra W. Russ (Washington, DC: American Psychological Association, 2013); and "Human Creativity: Its Cognitive Basis, Its Evolution, and its Connections with Childhood Pretence," by Peter Carruthers, *The British Journal for the Philosophy of Science* 53 (2002): 225–229.

25. Institute of Museum and Library Services, *Growing Young Minds: How Museums and Libraries Create Lifelong Learners* (Washington, DC: IMLS, 2013).

26. American Library Association Fact Sheet, "ALA Library Fact Sheet 17," 2014, www.ala.org/tools/libfactsheets/alalibraryfactsheet17.

27. New York Public Library, "NYPL Now!" (Summer 2014), https://www.nypl.org/sites/default/files/Now%20Summer%202014%20FINAL.pdf.

28. D. W. Swan, et al., *Public Libraries in the United States Survey: Fiscal Year 2011* (Washington, DC: IMLS, June 2014).

29. Valerie Gross, "Transforming Our Image through Words That Work: Perception is Everything," *Public Libraries* 29:5 (September/October 2009): 24–32.

30. Ibid.

31. Michael Gorman, *Our Enduring Values: Librarianship in the 21st Century* (Chicago and London: American Library Association, 2000).

part one

GET DIRTY

*"**BUT I'M NOT** really crafty."*

A lot of adult services librarians use this excuse to shy away from hands-on programs. You're not Martha Stewart, you say. You have vivid memories of gluing your fingers together during a macaroni project in first grade. There's a reason you didn't become a children's librarian.

"But I don't know anything about technology!"
Or perhaps you're a craft maven, but you find yourself making the same excuse for tech-based maker programs. You're not a coder. You were an English major. You've never touched an Arduino in your life, and you're pretty sure you'd electrocute yourself.

You are not off the hook for hands-on programs, crafty, technological, or otherwise. In fact, the worse your personal skills are, the better you may be at leading Get Dirty programs. You do not need to be an expert in order to run a playful hands-on program; even if you are, resist the urge to instruct and let your patrons take the lead.

The purpose of these programs is not to learn a specific skill or craft from an expert. They are not about memorizing by rote the most efficient way to produce a product. Your participants could do that just as easily by watching an online video from home. So why do they come to your events? Why are these programs likely to consistently be among your most popular? What are people learning, and why do they care?

These programs are, fundamentally, about learning to play. They are about diving in, getting messy, making mistakes, failing and starting over, laughing, and getting inspired all over again. This play space is where real, impactful learning happens. That kind of learning goes beyond how to make one single product, and instead teaches people to tap into their creativity. It builds their confidence in their own abilities, and inspires them to keep expanding their knowledge and playing with new ideas long after the class ends.

Styling yourself, or a presenter, as an "expert" who is teaching the "right" way to make something would actually stifle this creative play. Instead, make it clear from the beginning that you are learning right alongside your participants. Sure, you read some books and some instructions, and you've tested the project out once or twice. But that just makes you a guide, there for a little support. Your participants are becoming their own experts.

Begin each program by asking participants to share their own background or interest in the class. It is amazing how much diverse expertise you will find in the room! Create a space where each person can discover the incredible wealth of knowledge right there in their peers—and, just as important, recognize it in themselves.

The room setup for this type of program can significantly impact its success. It may be tempting to set up long tables facing forward, lecture-style, so participants can easily see any demonstration and have plenty of space to work. However, this classroom environment encourages solitary work and a focus on results that is antithetical to the real purpose and draw of Get Dirty programs. Instead, set up your tables in circles or squares, with a shared pool of materials in the middle. This arrangement emphasizes that the person demonstrating the project is not the "teacher," but is instead a coparticipant. It also encourages sharing, interaction, and conversation—maximum learning through maximum play.

Hands-on events are among the more expensive playful programs you may put on for adults. This makes it even more critical to be able to articulate their importance. Your funders need to understand that this type of programming is essential to meaningful adult education and the library's mission. Happily, this is not hard to do. Maker programs share the same fundamental values as public libraries.

When you help people learn to program a Raspberry Pi or sew on a button, you are empowering them to make choices that align their lives with their personal values. That is precisely the same reason we lend books. Our collections and services allow people to become their own experts. Our users can think, do, and create anything they can imagine, regardless of what is popular or pre-packaged. "Libraries are innately subversive institutions, born of the radical notion that every single member of society deserves free, high quality access to knowledge and culture," writes Dr. Matt Finch.[1] We put people in charge of their own learning by giving them the tools and access they need. Hands-on maker programs just update this enduring educational mission for today's world. And because they are both radically empowering and fun at same time, your patrons will adore them.

NOTE

1. Matt Finch, "Dirty Library Trilogy, Part 1: Drink Your Way to Better Librarianship," The Signal in Transition (December 30, 2012), http://matthew finch.me/2012/12/30/dirty-library-trilogy-part-1-drink-your-way-to-better-librarianship.

chapter one

Homemade Spa Products

GET FOOD ON your face! Raid your pantry to create these all-natural beauty products.

Community Need

Kitsap Regional Library first held this event in one corner of our sprawling county. We expected our audience to be a small group of adults who lived in the immediate area. Imagine our surprise when people started pouring in from the other end of the county, more than an hour away! Twentysomethings and thirtysomethings who never engaged with their own local libraries turned out to be more than willing to expend a significant amount of time and effort to attend a library program. They just needed an event that really appealed to them. The success of this program opened our system's eyes to the huge unfilled need in our emerging adult community for hands-on fun.

Source: Audrey Barbakoff, Kitsap Regional Library (WA)

What was it about this particular program that drew people in? In addition to the interactive appeal of any maker event, this one speaks strongly to two overlapping demographics common among emerging adults: the environmentally-conscious and the budget-conscious. Store-bought beauty products often include ingredients that some people wish to avoid. Even if their contents are pristine, their high prices can make them a rare luxury for those on an entry-level salary. A program that puts the consumer in control of what she puts on her body, while also making those products affordable, is a recipe for success.

This is an excellent holiday program, as it can easily be marketed as an opportunity to make your own gifts.

PROGRAM LENGTH	STAFF NEEDED	PREPARATION TIME	DIRECT COST
1 hour	1 person	1 hour	$100

MATERIALS

- Jars or other containers (2 per participant)
- Brown sugar
- White sugar
- Raw (turbinado) sugar
- Sunflower oil
- Vanilla extract
- Epsom salt
- Coarse salt
- Baking soda
- Essential oils
- Food coloring
- Bowls
- Spoons
- Measuring cups and spoons

PROCESS

Set out two large tables, one with the ingredients for Brown Sugar and Vanilla Scrub, the other with the ingredients for Relaxing Bath Salts. Position chairs so that each person has space to work, but conversation is still easy. Pull a collection of books on homemade spa products and make them available for participants to use for inspiration during the program or to check out after.

Give each participant a copy of the recipe handout (included). You can begin with a demonstration if you choose; however, because these projects are just simple mixing, this step may not be necessary. As with all programs in this section, make sure to draw out local expertise by starting a group conversation before diving in. It's amazing to hear people open up about their backgrounds and knowledge in areas like aromatherapy, cosmetics, or stress reduction. You are helping participants build a more resilient community by developing a rich network of local wisdom.

Then it's time to start mixing! Your job is to support conversation and experimentation as people work. Before you answer a question, encourage participants to try out solutions, answer each other, or consult books or websites. Inspire people to get creative in designing their own custom bath salt scents. Facilitate play and creativity whenever you can!

Further Reading

Coyne, Kelly, and Erik Knutzen. *Making It: Radical Home Ec for a Post-Consumer World*. Emmaus, PA: Rodale, 2010.

Gabriel, Julie. *Green Beauty Recipes: Easy Homemade Recipes to Make Your Own Natural and Organic Skincare, Hair Care, and Body Care Products*. Royal Tunbridge Wells, UK: Petite Marie Ltd., 2010.

Wolfer, Alexis, and Evan Sung. *The Recipe for Radiance: Discover Beauty's Best-Kept Secrets in Your Kitchen*. Philadelphia, PA: Running Press, 2014.

brown sugar and vanilla scrub

Ingredients

- ¼ cup brown sugar
- ¼ cup white sugar (or organic evaporated cane juice)
- 3 tablespoons raw sugar (or organic turbinado)
- 3 tablespoons sunflower oil (or olive oil, or really any skin-friendly oil without a strong scent)
- 1¼ teaspoons vanilla extract (or seeds from 1 vanilla bean, if you're feeling fancy)

Instructions

1. Measure and combine sugars.
2. Pack into sealable container or jar.
3. Pour 1/3 of the oil over the top. Wait a few minutes for it to settle. Repeat until your oil is used up. With the last of the oil, add the vanilla.
4. Stir well. Test the consistency; it should be a thick slurry that holds together. Adjust amount of oil and vanilla to your preference.
5. Seal and decorate!
6. Enjoy (or share the joy) soon! Homemade products with natural ingredients won't stay at their peak forever.

ADAPTED FROM RECIPES ON
- http://localkitchenblog.com/2010/12/17/homemade-body-scrub
- http://petitelefant.com/how-to-make-homemade-sugar-scrub

relaxing bath salts

Ingredients

- ½ cup Epsom salt
- ¼ cup Kosher salt, coarse sea salt, or other coarse salt
- 1–2 tablespoons baking soda, heaping
- Essential oil, as preferred
- Coloring, if desired

Instructions

1. Measure and combine salts and baking soda.
2. Choose an essential oil or combination of oils. Add five drops. Stir. Continue adding drops, one at a time, until scent reaches desired strength.
3. Add coloring, one drop at a time, stirring between additions, until salts reach desired color. (For candy-cane stripes, divide salts in half. Tint one half red; leave the other white. Layer carefully into jar in alternating stripes.)
4. Fill jar. Unleash your inner decorator!
5. Enjoy (or share the joy) soon! Homemade products with natural ingredients won't stay at their peak forever.

MORE GREAT IDEAS!
- **Crunchy Betty:** You have food on your face. www.crunchybetty.com
- **The Hip Girl's Guide to Homemaking:** http://hipgirlshome.com
- **Martha Stewart:** www.marthastewart.com
- **Not Martha:** www.notmartha.org

chapter two

Greener Cleaners

EMBRACE YOUR INNER mad scientist by mixing up cleaning products from grocery store ingredients.

Community Need

Do you know the first ingredient in most household cleaners?

It's water.

That might make anyone think twice before dropping six dollars on a bottle of name brand cleaner. Especially for people early in their careers and on a tight budget, a home brewed alternative made of cheap, common ingredients sounds pretty attractive.

Now add to that a growing concern among new adults about the potential health and environmental impacts of the chemicals we are exposed to every day. The green cleaners proliferating on store shelves might address this issue,

Source: Audrey Barbakoff, Kitsap Regional Library (WA)

but they come with their own set of problems. They may be far more expensive than standard cleaning products. And it can be difficult to tell which ones are merely "greenwashing" harsh cleansers—changing the labels and language to sound more sustainable, without significantly modifying the actual contents.

As with many of the other events in this section, this program draws in new adults with its fun, interactive blend of sustainability and affordability. That appeal exists throughout the year, but a little strategic timing can make your event more popular. Try it in March or April for spring cleaning season, or around the New Year for those making resolutions to be cleaner or greener.

PROGRAM LENGTH	STAFF NEEDED	PREPARATION TIME	DIRECT COST
1 hour	1 person	1 hour	$50

MATERIALS

- Water
- White vinegar
- Baking soda
- Rubbing alcohol
- Cornstarch
- Essential oils
- Spray bottles

PROCESS

In this program, participants will learn to make two cleaning products: an all-purpose cleaner and a glass cleaner. They use some of the same ingredients, so you may decide to set up both projects at one table for a small or medium-size group. If the group is larger, you might prefer to split into two separate tables. Make sure each person has space to work, but conversation is still easy. The fun in this program is as much about building community as it is about making a product. Display a selection of books on natural cleaners and make them available for participants during and after the program.

Actually creating these products is easy; just mix the ingredients together. The project's simplicity leaves plenty of time at the beginning for participants to get to know each other. Ask each of them to share their name, why they're interested in this program, and if they have any prior experience creating cleaning products. The diverse expertise in the room will amaze you! And better yet, it will lead to energizing, creative conversations among participants.

Have an assortment of essential oils on hand so participants can customize their own scents. Being able to make choices that reflect each person's personal preferences and values is a big part of what makes DIY programs fun.

Further Reading

A Bowl Full of Lemons: www.abowlfulloflemons.net.

Rapinchuk, Becky. *The Organically Clean Home: 150 Everyday Organic Cleaning Products You Can Make Yourself—the Natural, Chemical-Free Way.* Avon, MA: Adams Media, 2014.

Siegel-Maier, Karyn. *The Naturally Clean Home: 150 Super-Easy Herbal Formulas for Green Cleaning.* North Adams, MA: Storey Publishing, 2008.

homemade all-purpose cleaner

Ingredients

- 3 cups of warm water
- ½ cup vinegar
- 2 teaspoons baking soda
- 10 drops essential oil

Instructions

Add water and vinegar to the bottle. Make sure there is extra space, as the mixture will foam after the next step. Add baking soda. When reaction subsides, add essential oil as preferred. Note that vinegar is acidic, so test this cleaner before use on surfaces such as granite or marble.

White vinegar does not kill 100 percent of germs, so some situations may require precleaning with soap and water.

homemade glass cleaner

Ingredients

- 1 tablespoon cornstarch
- 2 cups warm water
- ¼ cup white vinegar
- ¼ cup rubbing alcohol

Instructions

Add the cornstarch to the bottle. Add other ingredients. Shake well.
Bonus tip: Wipe down glass with black-and-white newspaper for a streak-free shine.

chapter three

High-Tech Holiday Cards

WATCH SOMEONE'S FACE light up when you give them a homemade LED holiday card.

Community Need

Card making is a popular DIY around the holidays. While traditional crafts can be a draw for new adults, a standard card-making program at the library might get lost among similar offerings at craft and stationery stores, arts organizations, and private parties. How do you make yours stand out?

Integrating a little simple technology puts a spark into a perennial favorite. In addition to a creative and social crafting opportunity, this program offers a chance to learn a new skill in a safe environment. It gives even the most seasoned crafter a way to experiment with something a little different and discover some new techniques and tools. And it adds a modern edge to the homespun, a fun juxtaposition that always has its fans.

Source: Audrey Barbakoff, Kitsap Regional Library (WA)

The technology aspect also allows you to speak to an audience that other crafting programs might not catch. Just as crafters may enjoy learning more about technology, tech hobbyists can have fun stretching their artistic skills. Advertise at local makerspaces. Invite the employees of area tech companies. Don't be constrained by the stereotypical image of a crafter!

PROGRAM LENGTH	STAFF NEEDED	PREPARATION TIME	DIRECT COST
1 hour	1 person	1 hour	$50

MATERIALS

- LEDs in assorted colors
- Copper conductive adhesive tape
- CR1220 watch batteries
- Clear tape
- Card making supplies assortment, such as:
  - Scrapbook and construction paper
  - Glue, glue dots
  - Markers, paints, pens
  - Stamps
  - Stickers

PROCESS

Participants in this program are likely to have more experience with crafting cards than with wiring LEDs. If that is the case, start with demonstrating how to wire the card. This will help people think about how to incorporate the lights into their designs. You may also want to premake a demo card or two, so people can look closer as they work.

Fold a piece of paper in half to make the basic shape of the card. Poke a hole in the front and push the LED wires through to the inside. The LED has two wires, or leads. One is shorter than the other. Usually, the longer lead carries a positive charge, and the shorter one is negative. This is important because each face of the coin battery has a different charge. The positive wire must be connected to the positive side of the battery, and negative to negative. If you're not sure which way to set things up, there is an easy way to test. Just touch the LED to the coin battery, one lead to each face of the battery. If it doesn't light up, just flip the LED or the battery around.

Next, decide on the position of the battery inside the card. (A corner is generally best.)

Flatten the leads of the LED inside the card. Then run the copper adhesive tape from one lead to where the battery will go. Use regular gift-wrapping tape to secure the LED wire to the copper. Then use it to stick the battery down on top of the copper tape at the other end, making sure not to completely cover the face of the battery. Remember to double-check that you have the battery facing the right way up!

Next, you will run the copper tape for the second half of the circuit. However, do not connect this lead directly to the battery. Your goal is to line up the end of the tape so that it only connects with the battery when the card is closed. That way, the LED will light up when the card (and the circuit) is closed, and turn off when the card is opened.

Once people understand how to run the wiring, let them loose with the card crafting materials. Some participants will already have ideas for their designs. Others will get inspiration from their neighbors, from your samples, or from any card-making books you have in the room.

Make a card alongside your participants, and try not to jump in immediately if someone has a question. More often than not, people will figure it out themselves or with the help of a neighbor.

Don't forget to take pictures of the fabulous, creative results! And enjoy the excitement people feel as they learn something that's out of their comfort zone.

Further Reading

Dossis, Nick. *Brilliant LED Projects: 20 Electronic Designs for Artists, Hobbyists, and Experimenters*. New York: McGraw-Hill, 2012.

Gella. Let It Glow Holiday Cards. https://learn.sparkfun.com/tutorials/ let-it-glow-holiday-cards.

Instructables. Making an Electro Card Using Bare Paint! http://makeitat yourlibrary.org/technology/making-electro-card-using-bare-paint# .VbhPb7dcRpn.

chapter four

DIY Hot Cocoa Mix

WARD OFF CHILLY nights with customized hot cocoa mix. Enjoy all your favorite fixings, without preservatives or fillers.

Community Need

Just as new adults are interested in making affordable, sustainable, and personalized choices about the products they use, they want the same control over what they eat. At the same time, we are all busy people—we love convenience! It can be difficult to make those values walk hand in hand, but DIY hot cocoa mix does the trick. It provides a quick chocolate fix on a cold night, without high expense or unpronounceable ingredients.

But perhaps the real appeal of this project is as a gift. Custom cocoa mix is fast and inexpensive. At the same time, it is impressive and easy to customize for any recipient. To maximize your attendance, hold this program close to the winter holidays. The simplicity of this project also makes it perfect to pair with other activities. Try it as an all-ages event, or as part of a larger celebration with multiple activity stations.

Remember that personal choice is ultimately what makes this program playful. Following a recipe exactly can be hands-on and collaborative, but the real fun kicks in when everyone goes wild with personalizing their product. To make this as fun and engaging as possible, offer up a well-stocked toppings bar. Provide a wide variety of options, including some unusual ingredients. The more, the better!

This program is a good first foray for any librarian just getting started with hands-on events. It can be held in a short period of time in a small space. It requires very little preparation, is relatively inexpensive, and demands no skill beyond mixing a few things in a bowl.

PROGRAM LENGTH	STAFF NEEDED	PREPARATION TIME	DIRECT COST
30 minutes	1 person	30 minutes, mostly for shopping	$25–$50, depending on toppings and containers

MATERIALS

- Base recipe (required)
  - Unsweetened cocoa powder, natural or Dutch process
  - Powdered sugar
  - Powdered milk
  - Cornstarch
  - Salt
  - Decorative baggies or containers

- Toppings (optional suggestions; add or remove as desired)
  - Mini chocolate chips (dark, milk, and white)
  - Mini marshmallows
  - Crushed peppermint candy
  - Malt powder
  - Cinnamon
  - Chili powder
  - Instant espresso powder
  - Sprinkles

PROCESS

Lay out the base ingredients at the center of the table. Set up the toppings either on the table or in a row nearby. As always, include books or other materials for inspiration.

Walk participants through the base recipe as a group. The ingredients are simply measured out and mixed together, so this project does not need a demonstration. Just provide a handout with the recipe, and talk about what you're doing as you all create your base mixes. Share a few tips and tricks, and encourage others to do the same. For example, powdered sugar creates a smoother texture than regular table sugar, cornstarch will make the cocoa feel creamier and will help keep the mix from clumping, and salt helps bring out the flavor of the chocolate. Participants may want to share their own ideas for gluten-free, sugar-free, or vegan options.

Once everyone has their base created, let them at the toppings. Make sure they have a chance to share ideas for flavor combinations. Enjoy watching people get creative!

If you choose, you can also set up hot water and cups for people to try out their creations right there. This would work especially well if your cocoa station is part of a larger event. In that case, you could also include some toppings that would not store well in the dry mix. Examples include whipped cream, marshmallow fluff, or vanilla extract.

Further Reading

Brown, Alton. Hot Cocoa. Food Network. www.foodnetwork.com/recipes/alton-brown/hot-cocoa-recipe.html.

The Frugal Girls. Gifts in a Jar Recipes! TheFrugalGirls.com. http://thefrugalgirls.com/gifts-in-jars-recipes.

G&R Publishing. *Gifts in a Jar: Cocoas, Cappuccinos, Coffees & Teas: Recipes to Make Your Own Gifts*. Waverly, IA: CQ Products, 2002.

Stewart, Martha. Homemade Hot Chocolate. www.marthastewartcom/353001/homemade-hot-chocolate.

hot cocoa mix base recipe

Makes approximately 1 cup of cocoa mix

Ingredients

- 4 tablespoons cocoa powder
- 8 tablespoons powdered sugar
- 8 tablespoons powdered milk
- ¼ teaspoon cornstarch
- Pinch of salt

Instructions

1. Mix ingredients very well. Break up any clumps.
2. Make it your own! Add other flavors, like chocolate chips or peppermint, to taste. Crushed or shaved chocolate or chocolate chips will make the mix richer and creamier.
3. Add 2–3 heaping tablespoons to a standard size mug; fill with hot water or milk. Adjust amount of mix to taste.

ADAPTED FROM

- Alton Brown: www.foodnetwork.com/recipes/alton-brown/hot-cocoa -recipe.html.
- Smitten Kitchen: http://smittenkitchen.com/blog/2014/12/decadent-hot -chocolate-mix.

chapter five

Hypertufa Pots

HYPERTUFA IS A faux stone that is light, durable, and easily molded into nearly any shape. Start experimenting with the outdoor uses of this versatile material by making a small planting pot.

Community Need

Gardeners and artists abound in my county. Hypertufa is an excellent tool for both of these groups. It makes a durable, light pot for container gardening, and is easy to adapt for a wide variety of shapes and embellishments. In a community where nearly any garden or garden-art themed event or book is bound to be popular in the spring, why wasn't anybody playing with hypertufa?

Hypertufa, despite being very easy to create, can intimidate individual gardeners for two reasons. First, its main ingredient is cement. Many people have never worked with cement, and might incorrectly assume that it is going to be difficult or dangerous. Secondly, all of the major ingredients usually come in

Source: Audrey Barbakoff, Kitsap Regional Library (WA)

large quantities. A person wanting to experiment with a single pot is going to hesitate before buying the 50 pound bag of cement or 3 cubic-foot-square bag of peat moss available at the local hardware store.

One of my favorite reasons for hosting hands-on events is to teach people that they can do things they never thought possible. A program on hypertufa pots removes the mystery and fear around working with this material. Participants leave feeling empowered to go home and create more, to work together and share materials, and to explore their creativity in new ways.

PROGRAM LENGTH	STAFF NEEDED	PREPARATION TIME	DIRECT COST
60–90 minutes	1 person needed, 2 ideal (especially for clean-up!)	2 hours	$50–$100

MATERIALS

- Portland cement (NOT quick-drying)
- Perlite
- Peat moss
- Water
- Dust masks
- Gloves
- Large bucket
- Disposable plastic yogurt (or similar) containers, various sizes
- Nonstick cooking spray
- Rubber mallet
- Plastic bags

PROCESS

This is messy! First, make sure you and your participants feel comfortable getting themselves, and their space, dirty. Wear grubby clothes. Lay down tarps ahead of time, and make it clear that people don't have to be meticulously neat. You can model the way by getting your own hands dirty first. If you're happily elbow-deep in cement, everyone in the room will relax and join in. Safety note: Have all participants put on gloves and masks right at the beginning.

First, talk the group through the process of making hypertufa. Knowing what to expect helps people feel comfortable with what might be a new experience. Lay all the ingredients out for everyone to see, and give a quick walk-through. Explain what hypertufa is and why it's useful. Let people know the recipe—equal parts of all ingredients, mixing the dry and then the wet. Answer questions. (At this stage, questions are usually about where you found your ingredients. They are all common hardware store products.) More importantly, ask questions! Find out why people are there, what they want to learn, and what they have to share. You may be surprised to find artists, gardeners, and even some hypertufa experts. This event is participatory and creative—everyone learns and teaches together.

Get started mixing. Although each person could mix their own small batch of hypertufa, there are some significant advantages to mixing up one large bucketful as a group. It's fun! It gets everyone involved and talking together. Put a large bucket where everyone can see it. Ask a different participant to measure out and add each ingredient.

Add equal parts Perlite, peat moss, and cement to the bucket. Mix them together (your hands are the best tool for this!) breaking up any big clumps.

Slowly start adding up to one part water. You may not need this much, so go slowly and stop every now and then to mix it all up. Don't let it get soaked. When it's wet enough, it will feel like cottage cheese. It should stick together when squeezed, and drip a little water.

The mixture should sit for five to ten minutes at this point, which leaves you a great window to explain the next steps.

Each person needs two disposable containers, a large one and a smaller one. These are the molds for the pots. The large one will determine the size and shape of the outside of the pot, while the smaller one will make the hole for filling and planting. Give people a few minutes to look through the available cartons and choose what they like.

Once everyone has their two cartons, have them spray the inside of the large mold and the outside of the small mold with the nonstick cooking spray. This will make it easier to remove the finished product from the molds later.

Time to add the hypertufa! Let everyone dig in to the big bucket. Start by pressing some of the wet hypertufa mix into the bottom of the larger mold. Keep adding, working up the sides, until you have what looks like the right amount. Then gently push the small mold into the mixture. Add or remove hypertufa as necessary to get the desired shape.

Tap the outer container with a rubber mallet to push out air bubbles. Then finish the exposed rim of the pot as desired. Participants can leave it rough, smooth it with a finger, or even push in decorative stones or sea glass.

Wrap the pot in a plastic bag to hold in moisture. At this point, participants are ready to clean up and go home with their creations! The pots will continue to cure for twenty-four to thirty-six hours, until they are dry enough to remove from the mold. Some gentle tapping should do it, but the container can be cut away if needed. At that point the pots will be firm to the touch, but still not completely dry on the inside. They should be set in a dry place for two to three weeks before using. At that point, the makers can drill a hole in the bottom for drainage or sand the rim for an extra-smooth edge.

A few questions seem to come up frequently when I lead this program. People can't wait to start planning their own bigger, better projects at home! The first is about color. The wet hypertufa mixture is a dark gray, but when it dries it will pale to a light gray. Cement coloring is available commercially if people want to experiment with other colors. Also, this hypertufa may not be strong enough for large pots, birdbaths, or other bigger structures. To make it stronger, people can add acrylic fibers to the original mix.

Expect more laughing, talking, planning, and community-building than you've ever seen at a hands-off program. Be ready to make a mess and have fun!

Further Reading

Barbakoff, Audrey. "Radical Home Economics: Programs That Pop." *Library Journal* (April 8, 2014). http://lj.libraryjournal.com/2014/04/opinion/programs-that-pop/radical-home-economics-programs-that-pop/#_.

Lowe's Creative Ideas. Make Hypertufa Pots. www.lowes.com/creative-ideas/woodworking-and-crafts/make-hypertufa-pots/project.

The Martha Stewart Show. Hypertufa Pots. www.marthastewart.com/268962/hypertufa-pots.

Szuecs, Joe. "Hypertufa Planter: Maximum Zen for Minimum Yen." *Make: Projects.* http://makezine.com/projects/hypertufa-planter/.

chapter six

Bad Art Night

BREAK OUT THE glitter glue for an evening of creating truly dreadful art.

Community Need

alt+library is a project of Sacramento Public Library designed to reach twenty-somethings and thirtysomethings. Its fabulous programs often grow out of the personal passions of the librarians. When designing an event, they ask themselves: If I didn't work here, would I come to this? With craft maven Lori Easterwood (who now runs craft and vintage shop Make/Do) and art aficionado Jessica Zaker at the helm, Bad Art Night quickly became a staff and patron favorite.

Bad Art gives adults permission to turn off the self-judgment that stops us from just enjoying our creativity. Without any anxiety about being perfect—or even halfway decent—we can let our inner artist loose. "There is SO MUCH PRESSURE in your daily life to be successful, and having an event where you are celebrated for poor performance is a pretty huge relief," says Jessica. "Taking art classes, learning to sketch or paint, any hobby like that implies an intended success. And Bad Art night just lets you mess it all up. Adults get very little unscheduled play time. We need it."

If your adult patrons have lost their childhood excitement over gluing yarn to construction paper, Bad Art night reminds us that we are all creative and that we can all enjoy making things just for the sheer fun of it.

PROGRAM LENGTH	STAFF NEEDED	PREPARATION TIME
60–90 minutes	1 person	30 minutes

MATERIALS

- Terrible art supplies, such as:
  - Glitter, glitter, and more glitter
  - Pom-poms
  - Yarn
  - Stamps and stamp pads
  - Whatever you find in your children's librarian's stash
- Paint
- Glue
- Markers
- Construction paper, scrapbooking paper, wallpaper
- Canvases (or paper, if affordable canvases aren't available)

DIRECT COST

- $0–$25, depending on how many extra art supplies you have on hand, and if you offer prizes.

PROCESS

Setup for this program can be blissfully low-key. Just give people a space where they can be creative. Provide ample tables and chairs and access to a wide array of art supplies. Raid your music collection for some creativity-inspiring atmosphere. Decorate the room (terribly, please) if you have the time, inclination, and leftover hideous décor.

As your artists start creating, you might find that some are still feeling too much pressure to be "good." Encourage—or rather, discourage—them, so they can really let go and make terrible art. "That looks too real—add some pom poms!" suggests Jessica. Everyone will quickly get into the spirit. At one of the alt+library events, a participant chastised another, "Yours is too good." Someone else came to his defense, insisting "Well, he's trying to make it worse."[1]

After an hour or so of creating sad clowns, yarn poodles, and watercolor fart jokes, participants vote on the very worst piece of art produced that night. This gives everyone a chance to admire each other's creations. If you can, award the winner a prize—perhaps an art kit. Don't forget to take pictures! Or, if your fabulously awful artists are willing, consider displaying the pieces for a while.

The setup time and cost of this program are low, but the play factor is high. Give your adults some safe space to be ridiculous and watch them surprise themselves as they remember how creative they really are.

Further Reading

Sacramento Public Library. alt+library Meetup. www.meetup.com/altlibrary/.
Sacramento Public Library. Bad Art Night. http://altlibrary.com/tag/bad-art/.

NOTE

1. Ian Moore, "Sacramento Library Inspires Bad Artists," *Sacramento Press* (December 17, 2010), http://sacramentopress.com/2010/12/17/sacramento -library-inspires-bad-artists.

part two

GET OUT

"GO WHERE THE people are," advises *The Small but Powerful Guide to Winning Big Support for Your Rural Library*.[1] This is a potent idea for libraries of all sizes and locations. Unless your library has done some extensive community analysis, you may not have much data on your nonusers. But you know one thing about them for sure: they are not in your building. To engage them in library programs, lace up your shoes and go to them!

Have you ever put together a fantastic program, only to have nobody show up? Were you baffled and frustrated—even to the point of giving up—because you couldn't figure out why your carefully crafted event wasn't more popular? It might be because nobody knew it was happening. A key reason it is difficult to reach underserved populations like emerging adults is that they just don't know what we offer, no matter how hard we advertise.

Nonusers are often disengaged not just from the library but from many sources of community information. "Americans' library habits do not exist in a vacuum," concluded a Pew Internet study on library engagement.[2] "Many of those who are less engaged with public libraries tend to have lower levels of technology use, fewer ties to their neighbors, lower feelings of personal efficacy, and less engagement with other cultural activities." Our standard forms of advertising are not effective for many nonusers.

This may be particularly true for the group of new adults that Pew Internet has termed "Young and Restless."[3] Comprising 7 percent of the total population, these diverse, tech-savvy younger adults read frequently and have positive feelings toward the library. However, their engagement is low. Many are new to their communities, and "the defining feature of their current relationship with libraries" is that 85 percent do not even know where the local library is. In short, we have an incredible opportunity to reach these emerging adults. They like and care about libraries. They have a need for social connection that the library can fulfill. All we have to do is make it easier for them to find us.

Programs that get outside the building open up new avenues to reach this group. A partner location will spread awareness of our programs to its own customers in print, online, and through word of mouth. Because we are embedded in our potential users' environment, they do not need to visit a new place or make advance plans. They discover the library where they already are, framed in a way that appeals to them. Furthermore, this type of program often attracts the attention of local media, so a creatively located program can raise the profile of the library throughout the community.

You may not even have to design a new program to generate incredible outcomes. Even the most traditional programs can take on fresh appeal in a new environment. Some of the most successful examples in this chapter are simply program staples reinvigorated by their location or partner.

Just by walking out our front door, we gain access to large swaths of potential users who never realized that the library had something for them. And in doing so, we also give our existing fans a chance to get to know us in an entirely new way.

NOTES

1. American Library Association Rural, Native and Tribal Libraries of All Kinds Committee and American Library Association Office for Literacy and Outreach Services, *The Small but Powerful Guide to Winning Big Support for Your Rural Library* (Chicago: American Library Association, 2006).

2. Kathryn Zickuhr, Kristen Purcell, and Lee Rainie, From Distant Admirers to Library Lovers—and Beyond: A Typology of Public Library Engagement in America (Washington, DC: Pew Research Center, 2014), www.pewinternet .org/files/2014/03/PIP-Library-Typology-Report.pdf.

3. Ibid.

Book Group on a Boat
Ferry Tales

THIS FLOATING BOOK group meets monthly on board a commuter ferry.

Community Need

In Kitsap County, a significant number of adults regularly commute to work in Seattle by public ferry. The busiest route, a thirty-five minute sail between Seattle and Bainbridge Island, had a total ridership of 6,269,388 in 2013.[1] Many commuters pass the time by reading, but we realized we rarely saw those people in the library.

Because of their long hours and busy lives, many of these avid readers cannot easily make it to our building during open hours. But what if the library came to them, on their schedule? We decided to find out by starting a book club on board. This was an opportunity to give commuters access not only to great books, but also to a community of fellow book-loving riders. A close-knit group quickly developed. By embedding a librarian on the ferry, the library became relevant and accessible to this underserved population.

The benefits of getting out extended well beyond the monthly meetings. Once book club participants developed a relationship with a librarian onboard, they became full-fledged library supporters. They started seeking us out. Book club members registered for library cards, learned to download e-books, and started regularly attending library programs. (The ones on the weekend, anyway!)

Our community's reliance on public ferries is unique, but the plight of busy people traveling long hours to work is not. Any area with a significant population of regular commuters on public transit—boat, train, bus, or otherwise—may be able to use a similar program to reach them. Where do working adults gather in your community?

PROGRAM LENGTH	STAFF NEEDED	DIRECT COST
30 minutes–1 hour	1 person	$0

PREPARATION TIME

- Initial setup: 5–10 hours
- Ongoing: 1–2 hours monthly

MATERIALS

- 10+ copies of each title
- Set of 10 discussion questions

PROCESS

Once established, this program runs like a standard in-library book group. Each month, the participants read and discuss a book. The length of the discussion will vary with the duration of the ride; the Seattle-Bainbridge Island ferry takes thirty-five minutes, which is adequate time for a short, spirited discussion. On average, ten discussion questions will be more than enough to facilitate a thirty-minute to one-hour discussion. A sample set of discussion questions is included in this chapter. For questions specific to an individual title, consult the publisher's website.

Meeting on public transportation does present a unique set of logistical challenges. Pick a route busy enough to have regular commuters, but not so packed you will be unable to find a space. Stick with the afternoon commute, when people are more interested in relaxing and socializing than in the morning.

Make sure people can find you by establishing a standard meeting place. Look for a seating area well suited to discussion; participants should be able to face each other, ideally in an area that is visible but quiet enough for conversation.

Because of the nontraditional setting, the greatest logistical challenge is raising awareness of the program among its potential audience. Ferry Tales has a large banner to hang during the discussions, attracting attention. Consider drumming up interest in advance by riding along several times without a planned program, just to talk with people who might be interested and collect contact information.

Further Reading

Barbakoff, Audrey. "Words on the Water." 2012. Published electronically September 20, 2012. http://boingboing.net/2012/09/20/words-on-the -water.html.

LitLovers. "Reading Guides." www.litlovers.com/reading-guides.

Molaro, Anthony, and Leah L. White. *The Library Innovation Toolkit: Ideas, Strategies, and Programs*. Chicago: ALA Editions, 2015.

Discussion Questions

1. Overall, what did you think of the book? What made you like or dislike it?
2. What were your favorite moments in the book? Why did you enjoy them so much? Did any parts surprise you?
3. Who was your favorite character and why?
4. Which relationship in the book was most interesting to you? Why?
5. Did you identify personally with any of the characters, settings, or situations? How did they relate to your life?
6. Identify a few of the major symbols throughout the book. What do you think they represent?
7. How did the style of the book affect your experience of reading it? How do you think it would have been different if written in another style?
8. What do you think was the significance of the title?
9. What did you think of the ending? If you were writing the book, would you have ended it the same way?
10. Did you do any outside reading related to this book—perhaps about the setting, time period, or author? What did you learn?

NOTE

1. Downtown Seattle Association, Transportation, 2014, www.downtownseattle .com/files/file/Transportation042914.pdf.

Literary Pub Trivia
Books on Tap

BOOK LOVERS AND film geeks will dazzle each other with their genius at this monthly pub trivia game.

Community Need

In a small town with minimal nightlife, residents crave fun and social evening activities. Since the events that do happen in our community tend to focus on families and seniors, we thought that a nighttime event for emerging adults would fill a large unmet need. By making the program 21+ and holding it in a bar, we signaled to this underserved group that this event was truly for them.

Not only does Books on Tap build community among new adults, it engages them in the library's mission. Through literary trivia we are creating a space where talking about books and media is fun, social, and relaxing. Wanting to win each month motivates people to read books, watch films, and even brush

Source: Audrey Barbakoff and John Fossett, Kitsap Regional Library (WA)

up on local history. As they work their way through the booklists used for the trivia questions, they try out formats, genres, and authors they would not otherwise have read.

Books on Tap is a perfect example of the power of melding play with learning. Because team trivia makes reading and discussing books fun and social, it encourages people to read more frequently, deeply, and widely than they would for any less exciting program.

PROGRAM LENGTH	STAFF NEEDED
2 hours	1 person

PREPARATION TIME

- 1–4 hours per month
- The primary prep activity is writing the trivia questions, and the time that takes can vary. It may take several hours if done from scratch by a staff person. However, staff time can also be almost entirely eliminated. Writing questions is an excellent task for a well-read volunteer, and literary trivia questions can be easily found online.

MATERIALS

- Booklist with 25+ books and/or movies
- 4 rounds of trivia, 10 questions each

DIRECT COST

- $0–$25
- This cost is for prizes. They don't need to be elaborate, but everyone loves to be recognized and rewarded for winning. Used books from a Friends of the Library book sale work well. Local businesses may also be willing to donate small prizes. If you are considering purchasing prizes, be aware that you may not be allowed to use public funds. A Friends group or Foundation may be able to do this for you.

PROCESS

Books on Tap consists of four rounds of approximately ten trivia questions each. The questions are based on a list of books and films, which rotates roughly every six months. The list should include a few things participants are likely to have already read and a few things that will stretch them. You will also want to represent a variety of tastes. As a result, the lists should be diverse, including fiction and nonfiction, current best sellers and old favorites, light reads and serious commitments, books from across genres and periods and places, graphic novels, and even a few YA (young adult) and children's books.

Play happens in teams. Like most pub trivia games, players divide themselves up however they like. Teams do not have to be the same size. When a person arrives without a team, ask an existing smaller team to include the new player. They are generally very happy to welcome someone in, and often end up playing together regularly. New friendships can grow out of vigorous conversations about favorite books.

Make sure to begin the first round with easy, straightforward questions. Managing the difficulty level is critical to the program's success. If the trivia is too hard from the beginning, people will stop wanting to play. Excessively difficult questions early in the game have a clear, immediate negative impact on attendance. In addition to straightforward trivia, later rounds may include themes or games, such as matching a character to a book, identifying first or last lines, or answering questions based on images. One librarian in our system has started including a round of local history questions, written by the historical society.

Scoring is largely straightforward, but it can also be a place to insert a little drama or ease tension. In most rounds, one correct answer is worth one point. To keep lower-scoring teams engaged through the very end, correct answers in the final round are worth two points. Also, to mitigate any embarrassment over not knowing an answer, my games include "laugh points," or a half-point for an incorrect answer that makes me laugh. While celebrating the winner is important, prizes can be small or even nonexistent; the participants are coming for the game itself.

Meeting at a bar or restaurant opens up new opportunities for attracting players to your game. Our first partner, Treehouse Café, displays our posters and advertises the event on their own website. The library designed Books on Tap coasters, which the bar hands out even on nights when the game is not running. And of course, our loud laughter and gameplay attract attention from the Treehouse regulars, who came for a beer or a game of pool but decide to stay and play. This is a high-visibility program—heated discussions, cheers, and shouting are common—so just the act of holding it in an unexpected location is a surprisingly effective way to reach a new group of emerging adults.

Further Reading

Dillon-Malone, A. *Literary Trivia: Over 300 Curious Lists for Bookworms.* London: Prion, 2008.

Goodreads Trivia. https://www.goodreads.com/trivia.

Palmer, Alex. *Literary Miscellany: Everything You Always Wanted to Know About Literature.* New York: Skyhorse Publishing, 2010.

trivia questions

1. The following is the first line of what book? "I am an American, Chicago born—Chicago, that somber city—and go at things as I have taught myself, freestyle, and will make the record in my own way: first to knock, first admitted; sometimes an innocent knock, sometimes a not so innocent."

2. In what book does the narrator have three photos of ears taped above his desk?

3. In *The One and Only Ivan* by Katherine Applegate, Ivan makes a friend named Ruby. What species is Ruby?

4. In this book, our hero, still convalescing from a hangover, is summoned before his Aunt Dahlia and ordered by her to go to a particular antique shop and "sneer at a cow creamer." What is the book?

5. In *The Things They Carried* by Tim O'Brien, what unusual object does Henry Dobbins carry around with him for luck?

6. In *Embassytown* by China Mieville, the alien Ariekei are incapable of doing what?
   a. Speaking out loud
   b. Lying
   c. Using figures of speech

7. Which of these is true about John Elder Robison, author of *My Life with Asperger's*?
   a. He had an inflatable sex doll delivered to a junior-high teacher at school.
   b. He designed guitars that shot out rockets for the band KISS.
   c. He once tried to make friends with a girl by patting her on the head, because it had worked with his dog.
   d. All of the above.
   e. None of the above.

8. This book was first published in 1934 by the Obelisk Press in Paris, France, but this edition was banned in the United States. Its publication in 1961 in the United States by Grove Press led to obscenity trials that tested American laws on pornography in the early 1960s. What book is it?

9. In *The Hobbit* by J. R. R. Tolkien, what is the name of the dark and hostile forest in which Bilbo and the dwarves leave the path and are nearly killed?

10. In what book would you find the character Swede Levov?

Answers

1. *The Adventures of Augie March* by Saul Bellow
2. *A Wild Sheep Chase* by Haruki Murakami
3. Elephant
4. *The Code of the Woosters* by P. G. Wodehouse
5. His girlfriend's stockings
6. B
7. D
8. *Tropic of Cancer* by Henry Miller
9. Mirkwood
10. *American Pastoral* by Philip Roth

Book Club in a Bar
Books on Tap

WHAT'S BETTER THAN talking about books once a month? Talking about books over beer and french fries!

Community Need

When Leah White started working at Northbrook Public Library (IL), she noticed that her library had "great programs available for the very young and the very old but not a lot for the ages in between." She decided to create a program to reach adults ages twenty-five to fifty who weren't using the library. To engage this group, her program would have to make them see the library in a new way. So she decided to set her book group in a pub.

Source: Cathleen Doyle, Tracy Gossage, Mike Hominick, Leah White, Northbrook Public Library (IL)

One of the unique successes of this group has been its ability to evolve and adapt to the needs of its users. Although the program was successful right away—the first meeting drew twenty-seven participants, and the core group remains at sixteen to twenty-five several years later—Leah and her cohost Cathleen Doyle quickly saw that the demographic they had targeted was not exactly the one they were reaching. Most of the participants were at least forty years old.

Rather than try to change this, the library embraced it. The audience they did attract was a diverse group of people who had rarely or never used the library before. They ranged in age from the twenties to the seventies, and were equally divided between men and women. "In other words," says Tracy Gossage, a current facilitator for Books on Tap, "by trying to service one group we often don't see at our in-house discussions, we reached another group we don't typically see at in-house discussions."

Even as the facilitators have changed over the years (a challenge for any book group!), their dedication to meeting the needs of the people in front of them has not wavered. Many aspects of the group are put to a vote, and changes are welcome. For example, based on the participants' preferences, casual discussions of what each person was reading were replaced with the more traditional focus on a single monthly title. "Maybe it's because we meet outside the library, and more specifically at a restaurant/bar," noted Tracy, "but the people who attend seem more comfortable making suggestions and voicing their opinions."

Even as we do more work to understand our communities, programs may end up filling a different need or appealing to a different audience than we intended. That's fine! Keep asking your patrons what they want, and be willing to adapt to their changing needs.

PROGRAM LENGTH	PREPARATION TIME	DIRECT COST
1 hour (although members typically socialize before and after)	1 hour	$0

STAFF NEEDED

- 1–2 facilitators.
- Currently, Northbrook alternates monthly between two facilitators, Tracy Gossage and Mike Hominick, with a third, Cathleen Doyle, assisting every month.

MATERIALS

- Copies of monthly title
- Discussion questions

PROCESS

The mechanics of this group are similar to a traditional book discussion. Each month, the group meets at a bar/restaurant to discuss a specific title. You may want to select books outside of the normal book club fare. "The type of person who would attend is one who doesn't want to sit in a boardroom and drink decaf coffee while talking about *The Help*," explains Leah.[1]

That's not the only possible format for a group like this, but it is the one that worked best in Northbrook. Initially, months alternated between discussing a shared title and having an informal "Books and Brews" chat about what each person was reading. Ultimately, the participants voted to switch all months to discussing a single title. You can try out a few different discussion styles early on, or ask your participants what would work best for them.

Choosing a location is one of the most critical aspects for the success of this kind of group. First, address the logistical issues. Meetings need a comfortably large space where participants will still be able to hear each other. Also, since participants are purchasing their own food and drinks, make sure the establishment is willing to provide lots of separate checks.

The less concrete aspects of selecting a location are equally important. Who already gathers in the space? Does its personality—chain or local, pub or club—attract the demographic your group is targeting? Is it easy for people to get to after work, with good parking or access to public transit? Just as importantly, is the management receptive to the idea of working with the library? Will they be good partners and communicators? What kind of service will they provide to your participants while they're there? Maintaining a strong relationship with the right venue will be an important factor in your group's success.

As with any Get Out program, a book club in a bar gives you unique opportunities to promote the library to a new audience. Books on Tap meets at a pub near a train station, so the library hung posters in the station to attract commuters. This has proven to be one of their most successful sources of advertising for the group. Northbrook Public Library was also creative with advertising in their partner venue. Going beyond standard posters, they printed up some inexpensive coasters to hand out. They even made temporary tattoos! When you get out of your library, don't overlook the innovative advertising possibilities that open up for you.

Further Reading

Oak Park Public Library. Genre X. http://oppl.org/events-classes/genre-x.

Sacramento Public Library. Alt+Library Book Club. http://altlibrary.com/
altlibrary-book-clubs-2/.

White, Leah. "The Modern Book Club (Meets in a Bar)." *Letters to a Young Librarian* (2013). http://letterstoayounglibrarian.blogspot.com/2013/01/the-modern-book-club-meets-in-bar-by.html.

Books with Great Discussions at Books on Tap

Timothy Egan: *The Worst Hard Time*
John Green: *Looking for Alaska*
Chad Harbach: *The Art of Fielding*
Blaine Harden: *Escape from Camp 14*
David Mitchell: *Cloud Atlas*
Karen Thomas Walker: *The Age of Miracles*
Andy Weir: *The Martian*

NOTE

1. Leah White "Books on Tap: The Book Group That Meets in a Bar." *Marketing Library Services* (27, no. 5), www.infotoday.com/mls/sep13/White—Books-on-Tap—The-Book-Group-That-Meets-in-a-Bar.shtml.

chapter ten

Cookbook Book Group
Eat Your Words

TALK WITH YOUR mouth full. A cookbook group combines reading, cooking, and of course eating.

Community Need

Cookbooks are consistently among the highest circulating nonfiction at Kitsap Regional Library, as they likely are in many public libraries. Our librarians had often discussed ways to engage our cookbook readers with hands-on programs where they could cook, eat, and share their favorites. However, we always hit the same stumbling block: our space.

In order to prepare and serve food, our space had to meet a variety of health code requirements. Because our meeting room wasn't ideal for this kind of use, we would be limited in what we could do. The lines between what was acceptable and what wasn't were sometimes unclear. We also faced liability concerns, in case someone did get sick despite adhering to health code.

Source: Audrey Barbakoff, Kitsap Regional Library (WA)

When a new gourmet food business opened up in town, we saw our opportunity. This company wanted to become a community center for sharing and celebrating fresh, local foods. It combined a small selection of specialty ingredients, wines, and cookbooks with a commercial kitchen for classes, demonstrations, tastings, and the occasional meal. They needed foot traffic, publicity, and a way to foster a sense of community; we needed a commercial kitchen. Together, we launched Eat Your Words.

PROGRAM LENGTH	STAFF NEEDED
1 hour	1 librarian to facilitate the group; 1 chef

PREPARATION TIME

- 1 hour for the librarian
- 1–2 hours for the chef

MATERIALS

- Cookbooks
- Discussion questions
- A prepared dish from the cookbook

DIRECT COST

- $0–$100
- In our case, the partner business contributed the food and space, so the cost was $0.
- This may vary based on the partnership.

PROCESS

Once a month during the lunch hour, a group of cookbook enthusiasts gather to talk about a book. This is the usual librarian-facilitated book discussion, with a twist: while we talk, a chef prepares a dish from the cookbook for everyone to taste.

Discussing a cookbook requires a different type of question than most book club conversations. There may or may not be characters or a plot (though some cookbooks have one or both), and people don't necessarily read front-to-back, cover to cover. Here are a few tried and true discussion starters from this group:

- Did you make any recipes from the book? What did you think?
- What was your favorite recipe in the book? It can be one you've tried, or just the one that seems most appealing to you. Why does it sound so good?
- Did you encounter something—a recipe, a common ingredient, a combination—that you wouldn't normally eat? What is it, and did this book tempt you to try it?
- Have you made much of this type of food before? How was this book similar or different to others in the same genre? Did you like it more or less and why?

These questions work for nearly any cookbook. Then you can add a few that are specific to the particular book, based on its style, tone, personal touches, any narrative it includes, outside interviews with the author(s), or the reactions of reviewers.

My group tried out or considered several variations on this basic structure. When possible, we selected cookbooks by local restaurateurs and invited the chef/author to speak. Even if the author couldn't be there, comparing the experience of visiting the actual restaurant with using the cookbook always sparked discussion.

We also experimented with what we were reading. The group decided to read a food-related memoir a few times a year. We tried a few discussions around a theme, rather than a specific book. One month, for example, we might each bring a different Mexican cookbook. Another month, we all brought our own personal favorite cookbooks to share. And one particularly memorable month, we had a giant book launch party for a new cookbook memoir by a prominent local chef.

These or other formats might work better for your library, depending on your local partners. For example, our participants never got to cook their own food. Instead of having a chef prepare the dish, what if the participants all made something during the meeting? We also considered having people bring a dish they had prepared from that month's cookbook. Whatever the resources in your area, you can find a way to build a program that works for your local foodies. Who are the chefs, farmers, and food organizations in your community? How could you work with them to combine books, cooking, and eating?

Further Reading

Brickman, Sophie. "Recipe for a Better Book Club; When Cookbooks Are the Focus, the Benefits of Membership Are Tangible (and Tasty)." *Wall Street Journal Online* (May 24, 2013). www.wsj.com/articles/SB10001424 127887324787004578495130943486190.

Library Journal. "Cooking Reviews." http://reviews.libraryjournal.com/ category/books/nonfic/sci-tech/.

Steenson, Julie. "Program Model: Cookbook Challenge." *Programming Librarian* (November 19, 2015). www.programminglibrarian.org/programs/ cookbook-challenge.

Velden, Dana. "Good Idea: Start a Food Lit or Cookbook Book Club." *The Kitchn* (February 8, 2010). www.thekitchn.com/good-idea-start-a-food -lit-or-108115.

chapter eleven

Book-to-Action

MAKE A DIFFERENCE in your community with literature. This series of programs combines book discussions with real-world service projects.

Community Need

We all know reading can change lives. Often this happens in subtle, long-term ways. But in a Book-to-Action group, literature motivates service projects that quickly and directly improve the lives of people in your community. Whatever the social justice issues in your area, you can tailor Book-to-Action to engage people in learning, discussion, and hands-on involvement around those themes.

The social justice aspect of this group can be particularly meaningful for emerging adults, as it fulfills their mounting need for civic and community engagement. In a recent poll, 29 percent of adults under thirty agreed that volunteering was a "very important obligation," a significant increase from 19 percent in 1984. In 2013, 22 percent actually volunteered, up from 14 percent in 1989.[1] In its role as community connector, the library can help new adults get involved locally with the issues they care about. At the same time, the discussions and projects bring people together, connecting them more deeply with the community they discuss and support. It's no wonder that participants have called the Book-to-Action experience "'motivating,' 'empowering,' 'uplifting,' 'powerful,' and 'thought-provoking'."[2]

Combine the power of reading with the chance to give back, and discover a way to fill multiple community needs at once—and have fun doing it!

STAFF NEEDED	PREPARATION TIME	MATERIALS	DIRECT COST
1–2, plus a dedicated community partner	Varies	Copies of the selected title	$0–$250

PROGRAM LENGTH

- 2–7 hours (spread out over 1–3 events)
  - Book discussion: 1 hour
  - Author visit: 1–2 hours
  - Service project: 1–4 hours

PROCESS

Book-to-Action has four elements: read a book, discuss it with a group, meet the author (if possible), and take action. The structure and topics within that framework are very flexible, allowing any library to do what works best for them and their community.

First, select a book with a theme clearly related to a social issue facing your community. It may be fiction or nonfiction, as long as it engages the reader with the topic. If you already have a topic in mind, reach out to a few community organizations that work with this issue. Ask for their input or partnership in selecting the book and beyond. If you already know your title, still identify and contact local organizations as soon as possible.

Bring people together for a book discussion where they can grapple as a group with the questions and problems the book raised for them. Increase public interest by inviting a speaker, such as the author or a relevant community activist. Finally, bring people's new knowledge and passion to life with a short (up to one day) community service project outside of the library.

These elements can be broken out into multiple events or condensed into just one or two. For example, a large library system that wanted to promote Book-to-Action for the whole community might hold multiple book discussions, a separate author visit, and a large service project, all over the course of a month or more. A library wanting a smaller undertaking might simply invite a speaker to the book discussion and follow that immediately with a couple hours of volunteering nearby.

Choose a theme that will resonate with the emerging adult audience you are trying to reach. Not sure what issues they are passionate about in your community? That's no problem—you will need to find and work closely with a community partner in this project. Look for an organization working locally on social issues that already attracts people in your target audience. Are your area's new adults volunteering at animal shelters, writing checks to international aid organizations, or protesting environmental destruction? Identify the issues they are passionate about and then find a partner doing meaningful work in that area. Not only will a partner help you select a meaningful book, plan supporting events, and give you a direct connection to the audience you hope to reach, they will be the hosts for your service project.

If you're still not sure how to choose from the countless permutations of possible books, partners, and projects, take inspiration from some of the libraries that have held Book-to-Action groups since Multnomah County Library debuted the idea in 2008. Solano County Library paired *Twelve Steps to a Compassionate Life* by Karen Armstrong with volunteer shifts at an anti-poverty Opportunity Conference. Hayward County Library read *Farm City* by Novella Carpenter, which mobilized three hundred volunteers to replant a school vegetable garden. Sonoma County Library chose *A Dog's Purpose* by W. Bruce Cameron, then spent half a day cleaning up the local dog park. California State Library's Book-to-Action Toolkit provides a long list of suggested combinations.

Further Reading

California State Library. Book-to-Action. www.library.ca.gov/lds/getinvolved/booktoaction/.

Get Involved: Powered By Your Library. "From Book to Action: One Library's Story." 2012. https://www.youtube.com/watch?v=tOkDOYR5Pb4.

Thomas, Sally. *Book-to-Action Toolkit*. 2012. www.library.ca.gov/lds/getinvolved/booktoaction/docs/Final-Toolkit-large.pdf.

NOTES

1. *Philanthropy News Digest*, "More Millennials Value Volunteering Than Previous Generation Did," *Philanthropy News Digest* (January 5, 2015), http://philanthropynewsdigest.org/news/more-millennials-value-volunteering-than-previous-generation-did.

2. Sally Thomas, *Book-to-Action Toolkit* (California: California State Library, 2012), www.library.ca.gov/lds/getinvolved/booktoaction/docs/Final-Toolkit-large.pdf.

chapter twelve

Book Bike
Spoke & Word

THIS BIKE AND trailer combination "pops up" in events around the community, where sources agree—it's even cooler than the ice cream cart.

Community Need

Even with twenty-eight locations and four bookmobiles, San Francisco Public Library staff knew they were not reaching everyone in their community. In a concern familiar to public libraries of all sizes, many people still don't realize how much the library has to offer them. So the librarians found a new way to spread the word: on two wheels. The book bike puts the library "where people naturally gather," from farmers' markets to baseball games to the Pride Parade, says Christy Estrovitz, SFPL youth services manager and book bike coordinator.

Source: Christy Estrovitz, San Francisco Public Library (CA)

Pedal-powering their resources is a fantastic way to heighten the library's visibility. A bike can go places a large bookmobile can't easily access, especially with San Francisco's topography and parking challenges. The eye-catching trailer is a conversation starter for library users and nonusers alike. And it's a perfect medium for featuring the digital books, magazines, and movies that may appeal to people who don't visit a physical library. City Librarian Luis Herrera reflects, "What a joy ride for our staff to ably serve our community on the go—from neighborhood fairs, to parks and festivals, Spoke & Word is a marketing and outreach sensation!"

The book bike appeals to a variety of ages, but some pop-up events are tailored specifically to twentysomethings and thirtysomethings. For example, librarians recently brought the bike to Chronicle Books headquarters, where many young professionals work. They combined a celebration of a recent partnership with a library card registration drive. Thirty adults signed up for new cards, and Chronicle employees got to meet their local branch librarian. The librarians followed up the visit with an online connection, posting pictures to Twitter and Instagram.

Next up: a visit to Nerd Night at an area bar. The self-identified nerdy young professionals who attend "might not be library users because they still think of the library as only being books," says SFPL employee Tim Lucas. They "don't know all of the other amazing things the library has to offer them from the comfort of their own homes."

At least, not until the book bike rolls up to show them.

PROGRAM LENGTH

1–2 hours

STAFF NEEDED

- 1–3 people
  - 1 coordinator to handle scheduling, training, and maintenance
  - 1 person on the bike, such as the local librarian (may be the same as the coordinator)
  - 1 additional person accompanying the rider for support and safety at the event (optional)

PREPARATION TIME

- 1–3 hours
  - 2 hours for training for new users
    - 1 hour rules of the road training
    - 1 hour to review the user guide to learn how the bike and trailer work
  - 1 hour prep for specific event

MATERIALS

- Bike (with electric assist, if possible)
- Trailer
- Wi-Fi hotspot
- Laptop
- Barcode scanner
- Books, circulating and/or giveaway
- PR materials and handouts
- Bubble machine

DIRECT COST

- $5,000–$15,000
- SFPL's bike and trailer are highly custom, designed by Burgeon Group to look like a "mini airstream." The product that came from this collaboration, and others like it, can run up to $10,000. You may be able to find a grant to help subsidize this cost—look around!
- Local craftspeople might be able to help you create something similar for significantly less. If you are considering building your own solution, Christy recommends keeping a few considerations in mind. Make sure the trailer is aerodynamic and light enough to be moved easily on a bike, and that it will still stand up when detached. It needs to fit inside one of your library's vehicles, and through doorways. Also, the electric assist bike is a significant expense, and one you may be able to skip if you live in a flat area. Christy estimates that this could be done for about half the price of the commercially purchased trailer.
- One place not to skimp? The bubble machine! Adding one on is inexpensive, and it draws a lot of interest to the book bike.

PROCESS

Spoke & Word is a trailer connected to an electric assist bike. Bright and attention-grabbing, the trailer is equal parts PR piece and mobile service point. When parked, both sides open out to create display shelving. SFPL uses this space primarily to let people know about their digital offerings, such as downloadable magazines through Zinio, streaming video through Hoopla, and their Bibliocommons app. They may also add books or other content tailored to a specific event or audience. Inside, the trailer contains a WiFi hotspot, two USB docking stations, space to safely carry a laptop and barcode scanner, book and material storage, and even a bubble machine. An external holder supports a large, brightly colored umbrella. Underneath it, librarians spread out folding furniture and blankets to create a reading nook.

The entire assembly is stored at the Central library, but any trained staff member in the system can reserve it. This shared model allows the book bike to reach the broadest possible variety of events and communities. A coordinator oversees its schedule and upkeep. Christy spends about 5 percent of her time in this role. She answers questions and provides support to staff using the bike, runs monthly maintenance checks, and handles check-in and cleaning after events. More generally, she talks with staff to make sure the bike continues to meet library and community needs.

Partnerships are crucial to the success of the book bike. They allow it to accomplish its mission of reaching people where they already gather. Often this means visiting existing events and community spaces. But it can also mean leading

events and inviting partners in. For example, the book bike inspired the library to take the lead in a Family Biking Showcase. Various organizations brought interesting and unusual bikes for visitors to try out. The bike enthusiasts this event attracted were a population that might not otherwise seek out the library.

The nimble nature of the bike lets the library take advantage of serendipitous connections. While out on Spoke & Word, one staff member noticed a large crowd gathered at a nearby school for an outdoor event. On the spot, the staff member brought the bike over and stayed for a forty-five-minute pop-up. These spontaneous interactions can also be one-on-one. Christy loves to bike by coffee shops, bike paths, and other public places where people stop her to ask questions. This leads to "candid conversations I would never have on my own bike," she says, and the "natural joy of having those conversations on the street, and bringing people back to the library."

Moving forward, SFPL will be considering ways to staff the bike more efficiently. Although they worked hard to get buy-in before debuting the bike, even the most invested employee's time is limited. They have already shifted from utilizing only their mobile services department staff to allowing any employee to train to use the bike. But are there creative solutions that could make even better use of valuable staff time? Would interns or volunteers help? SFPL's staffing model is still evolving, and Christy recommends thinking seriously about your staffing capacity for the bike from the very beginning.

Despite the expense and time, this immediately successful project was worth the investment at SFPL. "There's no better way to start the work day," Christy says. "It's one of my favorite projects of the last few years."

Further Reading

Davis, Paul M. "The Book Bike." *Shareable* (April 20, 2010). www.shareable.net/blog/the-book-bike.

Francis, Chris. "Custom Library Book Bikes Roll Out Across US." *American Libraries* 45, no. 6 (June 2014): 18–19.

Johnson, Lizzie. "Spoke & Word Bike Takes S.F. Library to the Streets." *San Francisco Chronicle* (July 24, 2015). www.sfchronicle.com/bayarea/article/Spoke-Word-bike-takes-S-F-library-to-the-6404867.php.

San Francisco Public Library. "S.F. Public Library Rolls Out New Book Bike Named Spoke & Word." April 17, 2015. http://sfpl.org/releases/2015/04/17/s-f-public-library-rolls-out-new-book-bike-named-spoke-word/.

Shank, Jenny. "Bright Orange 'Book Bikes' Signify Changing Times for Libraries." *MediaShift* (September 24, 2014). http://mediashift.org/2014/09/bright-orange-book-bikes-signify-changing-times-for-libraries/.

part three

GET TOGETHER

WHICH SOUNDS LIKE more fun?

- Learning to knit by watching a YouTube video or by joining your best friend's monthly Stitch and Bitch?
- Playing a game by yourself or by forming alliances and rivalries across the network or the tabletop?
- Falling in love with a great book nobody else is reading or falling in love with a great book and then discovering that a giant convention of its devoted fans is happening next week?

Some things are simply more fun when we do them together. And more fun means more engaging, more educational, more impactful. That's why even the most stalwart introvert will likely find that some of his most lasting life lessons involve another person—a parent, a small group of close friends, a teacher, or even just a book character so real it might jump off the page.

Without delving too deeply into the history of developmental psychology, scholars have known for decades that our peers, our teachers, our community, and our culture have a profound effect on how we learn. Theories recognizing the social context of learning have been appearing since the 1960s.[1] Play researcher Scott Nicholson notes that by improving social connections, gaming "helps [patrons] feel the library is relevant to their lives."[2] Multiple brain studies over the past twenty years have indicated that "emotions and content learning work together to produce a result that cannot be obtained separately or independently."[3] "Allowing adults to break free of their critical thinking and ordinary experience can jolt them into a new awareness that changes their perspective and allows for greater insights," reflects Dr. Scott Barry Kaufman.[4] (Kaufman made this statement in support of a preschool-style experience for adults. Fun program idea, anyone?) Great learning—and great library programs—are social.

Not only do social programs enhance engagement (and therefore fun and learning), they're easy to tie to your library's mission. Libraries are community builders and connectors. We are one of the last places where people from all walks of life gather together. We are third places and builders of increasingly-rare bridging social capital.[5] There's a very good chance that the word *community* appears directly in your public library's mission statement or features prominently in your long-range plans. "Building community" is a phrase likely to resonate with your manager, director, and board.

Best of all, it's simple to add or play up a social element in many library events. Consider the programs in the first two chapters of this book. "Get Dirty" programs teach hands-on skills, but anyone with an Internet connection or a book could easily learn those skills at home. "Get Out" programs focus on being in places where people already spend time; they don't need a library program in order to go there. So why do people come to our programs, often again and again? Human connection. It's the special sauce for fun, enriching events.

While the programs in this chapter are ones where the social element is the primary draw, don't forget to think about the social dimension you could add to any program. How can you make your maker programs, your outside-the-building (and the box) programs, and especially your classic staple programs like book groups and lectures, more social?

NOTES

1. Examples include Albert Bandura's Social Learning Theory and Lev Vygotsky's Social Development Theory.
2. Scott Nicholson, "Games in Libraries: Myths and Realities," *NYLA Bulletin* 56:4 (2008): 3.
3. Rocío Dresser, "Reviving Oral Reading Practices with English Learners by Integrating Social-Emotional Learning," *Multicultural Education* 20.1 (2012): 45–50.
4. Irene Chidinma Nwoye, "Meet the Two New Yorkers Who Are Starting a Preschool for Adults," *The Village Voice* (January 30, 2015), http://blogs.villagevoice.com/runninscared/2015/01/meet_the_two_new_yorkers_who_are_starting_a_preschool_for_adults.php.
5. Ray Oldenburg, *The Great Good Place: Cafés, Coffee Shops, Bookstores, Bars, Hair Salons, and Other Hangouts at the Heart of a Community* (New York: Marlowe, 1999); Robert D. Putnam, *Bowling Alone: The Collapse and Revival of American Community* (New York: Simon & Schuster, 2000).

chapter thirteen

A Library Murder Mystery
Dying for Love

HAVE A KILLER good time with a night of live-action murder and mayhem.

Community Need

The idea for this program came from a brainstorming session about Valentine's Day. We wanted to create a fun, free event for emerging adults that would be welcoming to both couples and singles. That meant we needed to avoid annoying sappiness without becoming too negative. It was also important to us to provide people with an alcohol-free option on an evening traditionally soaked in red wine.

Dying for Love, a murder mystery in the library, struck the perfect balance. The focus on love and murder was a tongue-in-cheek nod to the holiday that we hoped would appeal to emerging adults' sense of humor. Couples, families, singles, or teams could participate, so it offered a perfect opportunity for a date without any pressure to have one. Plus, this program was unique enough to drum

Source: Audrey Barbakoff, Kitsap Regional Library (WA)

up interest—it stood out from the chocolate tastings and prix-fixe dinner menus as a different way to have a great time.

In fact, the need for a program like this turned out to transcend age. While adults in their twenties and thirties did come, our murder mystery attracted people of all ages. Three generations of family played together; groups of teens teamed up; middle-aged women got babysitters and came with friends. In this case, the age diversity enriched the experience for everyone and did not discourage emerging adults from coming or from returning for future murder mystery programs.

PROGRAM LENGTH

2 hours

STAFF NEEDED

- At least 2 present for the night of the program, and ideally at least 1 more for setting up in advance of the program. Prior to the event, 5 people to play the suspects in short, prerecorded videos.

PREPARATION TIME

- 10–15 hours
- Preparation time for these programs is significant. Adult murder mysteries are high-interest, high-visibility special events with a significant payoff, but they require significant commitment as well.
- The time you choose to put in may vary significantly. The bulk of the time is spent transforming the familiar library into the new scene of a crime. The more complete and detailed each scene is, the more fun participants will have. Filming suspect statements and confessions can go quickly with no costumes, props, or background, or you can make them as elaborate as you choose. The more time you can put into this, the better it will be.

MATERIALS

- Set pieces and props for each scene (see Process for descriptions)
- Clues (see Process for full list of clues)
- 5 prerecorded suspect statement videos (1–3 minutes each)
- 5 prerecorded confessions (1–3 minutes each)
- Laptop and projector to show videos
- Programs with descriptions of suspects and victim (see Process for text)

DIRECT COST

- $0–$50
- The cost will vary depending on how the sets, props, and costumes are procured. In my library, this program had no direct cost because all the pieces were borrowed from staff, found in the basement, or plundered from the youth services supply closet. We did choose to provide light refreshments, at a cost of about $25.

PROCESS

Establish the Premise

Leave yourself at least a full hour from the closing of the library to the start of the program. Use this time to transform your space from a mild-mannered library to the scene of a deadly crime!

When guests begin to arrive, gather them together in a central spot or meeting room. Don't let them get close to the scenes and clues just yet! First, you want to establish the premise so they understand how to play the game and what to look for. Once most people have arrived, set the scene for the evening with a speech like this:

"Welcome to this special Valentine's Day weekend production by Library Theater! We're so glad you could come.

However, there's been a change of plans this evening. You were supposed to watch a romantic and heartrending drama by our skilled local actors and crew, but something terrible has happened! The star actor, Austin Jane, has been murdered—stabbed through the heart. He was killed right on the stage during our final rehearsal just moments ago. The lights went out, there was a scream, and when the lights came on, Austin was dead with a knife in his heart! All the actors and crew had an opportunity, so they have been taken to the police station for questioning.

But as library users, everyone knows you have the sharpest minds in town. The police want your help. You must search the library for clues. There are a few areas around the library that the theater was using heavily, so you may want to start there. But don't forget about the rest of the library—you never know where a deranged and desperate murderer may have left clues!

There are a few ground rules to observe. The suspects had no access to [fill in any areas patrons shouldn't go, like staff areas, another floor of the library, etc.], so we won't be searching there. Also, when you find a clue, please put it back as you found it, so other sleuths can draw their own conclusions!

Are there any questions?

When the police have finished taking the suspects' statements, we will gather together again and hear from them.

Make sure you take a program that was meant for the performance tonight. It will help you as you try to figure out who has done this terrible deed!

Good luck! I will let you know when the suspects' statements have been taken."

Participants pick up a copy of the program from the theater production that was "supposed" to happen that night. It has photographs and short bios of the cast and crew—the victim and the suspects. It reads:

ACTORS

- **Austin Jane**, our star! The dashing gentleman is a well-known actor with good looks, charisma, and a way with the ladies. Sorry girls, he is married to our director, Bea Goode. His favorite book is *Gone with the Wind* by Margaret Mitchell.
- **Holly Wood**, beautiful young ingénue. Our lovely leading lady has recently joined the company. Her favorite book is *Good in Bed* by Jennifer Weiner.
- **Hugh Mann**, supporting actor. The company can't imagine what we would do without Hugh there to play all our bit parts in every production! He would like to thank his sister Anita for always supporting him and for serving as a volunteer usher. He likes to listen to Shakespeare on audiobook.

PRODUCTION CREW

- **Bea Goode**, director and producer. The wife of our esteemed star, Austin Jane, is sadly directing her last production with us! Her favorite book is *Divorce & Money: How to Make the Best Financial Decisions During Divorce* by Violet Woodhouse.

- **Justin Thyme**, stage manager. He can usually be found wearing all black, staring intently at his script of the play. Thanks to Justin for taking the lead and keeping all our productions running smoothly. He would like to thank Holly for inspiring him every day. His favorite book is *The Remains of the Day* by Kazuo Ishiguro.
- **Anita Mann**, volunteer usher. She would like to thank Austin Jane for uplifting the souls of so many with his brilliant performances. Thank you, Anita, for never missing a single show or rehearsal! Her favorite book is *Tess of the D'Urbervilles* by Thomas Hardy.

SEARCH FOR CLUES

The participants can now search the library for clues. The librarian will have set up three scenes, each with clues and red herrings hidden inside. People may search them in any order. The scenes are:

- The crime scene (the stage)
- The dressing room
- Backstage

Clues are also hidden in the library stacks.

Decorate each scene to make it look as realistic as possible. The clues that must be concealed in each scene are:

THE CRIME SCENE (THE STAGE)

Chairs are set around a stage set up for a performance. A small stage or a rug designates the performance area. Set up the onstage "scene" how you like, perhaps with a small sofa and a table with a lamp. A curtain is a big bonus!

On the stage there is a masking tape outline of a body.

1. Near the outline of the body is a blackmail note, folded to imply it fell out of Austin's pocket. It says "I found your letter. I know what you did. Give me what I want or I will tell the world." The letters are cutouts from a magazine, pasted on.
2. The blackmail note is clipped to a letter from Holly. The letter has been torn up and taped back together. It says:

Dearest Austin,

I'm so glad we found each other. It's a dream come true. I know you don't want your wife to find out yet, so I understand that we must keep our meetings secret. It's hard, but I feel like I have already waited my whole life; I can wait a little longer.

Let's meet at the library on [fill in the date of your event] at [fill in a time a few hours before your event].

All my love,
Holly

3. A "bloody" knife [ketchup works fine] sits by the body.
4. A photo of Holly with Austin at the library, being used as a bookmark in Bea's favorite book, which she left in her purse under her chair in the audience.

BACKSTAGE

This area has a podium and stool for the stage manager, as well as the prop table. The stage manager's podium has his headset and anything else he'll need while calling the show—maybe a bottle of water, for example. The prop table is plain and utilitarian, with spaces taped out and labeled for each prop. Backstage, junk is scattered around— ladders, cables, old props, and costumes, etc.

1. Justin's script is on his podium. He has doodled Holly's name all over it with little hearts.
2. A knife is missing from the prop table. (Squares are taped out on the table for each prop; each square is labeled with masking tape. The square for "Knife" is empty.)

THE DRESSING ROOM

Each character has his or her own space, labeled with a name tag. This area is much more sumptuous than the backstage scene. Mirrors, costume pieces, jewelry, makeup, etc., hang on the walls and sit on the tables, revealing a little bit about the personality of their users. There is a wastebasket at each station.

1. In Hugh's dressing room space there is a program with "Austin" crossed out and "Hugh" written in to the starring role.
2. In Holly's area there is a letter from Holly to an agency that helps find birth parents. It lists her age—25.

3. In Austin's space, you find a printout of increasingly desperate love e-mails from Anita to Austin. Attached is a post-it that reads "enough for restraining order?"

THE STACKS

You don't need to do anything to change the appearance of your stacks.

1. Stuck inside an audiobook of Shakespeare there is a magazine page with letters cut out.
2. A photograph of an infant girl is found in *Tess of the D'Urbervilles*. It is dated twenty-five years ago.
3. *The Remains of the Day* and *Good in Bed* are on the shelf, but contain no clues.
4. You don't find *Divorce & Money*, because it's in Bea's purse at the crime scene.
5. *Gone with the Wind* is missing from the shelf.

HEAR FROM THE SUSPECTS

Let the participants explore freely, until most people seem to have found the majority of the clues. This may take between thirty minutes and one hour, depending on how many people are playing and how elaborate the scenes are.

When players are done searching, announce that the police have the suspects' statements ready. Call everyone back together in a room or space with a projector. These statements will be short videos recorded in advance, with suspects played by staff members or volunteers.

Before playing the videos, say:

"Good work discovering the clues! But before you decide who is guilty, let's hear what the suspects have to say. Maybe they can explain the incriminating evidence you uncovered."

JUSTIN: I can't believe you even suspect me—I've been keeping this company running smoothly for years! You're right, I am in love with Holly. And I was furious when I found that letter about Austin's secret meetings with her. He's just going to break her heart, like he does to every woman! I can't stand to see her hurt, and I would do anything to protect her. I was so furious that I ripped up the letter and threw it in the trash in the dressing room. But I'm not the blackmailer, I swear! If I were going to use the letter as blackmail, why would I rip it up the first place? And the killer has to be the blackmailer, right?

Does anybody suspect Anita? Anita, what do you have to say for yourself?

ANITA: I would never have hurt Austin! I loved him! We were high school sweethearts twenty-five years ago, you know. I was his true love. I mean, sure, he left me very suddenly back then, for some Little Miss Perfect. But when I heard about his divorce with Bea, I knew it was our chance to be together again! We have so much in common. Actually, one very important thing . . . but I don't want to talk about that. Anyway, he might have seemed a little hesitant in those e-mails, but I know he would have come around. Once I told him about . . . well, never mind. But he would have realized that I'm the only one for him, I'm sure of it. Holly must have done it! She knew she was going to lose Austin to me, and she couldn't stand that.

HUGH: Justin accidentally threw the pieces of that letter into my trash can. I taped it back together so I could read it. So what? And then I realized it was my chance at the big shot. Maybe I could blackmail Austin into not auditioning for the lead role in our next show. And then it would finally be mine! Plus, it was a nice chance to get back at Austin for breaking my sister's heart. Can't he see what he's doing to her? When he left her in high school, she had to go away. She was gone for nine entire months. She won't talk about it, but obviously she had some kind of nervous breakdown from it all.

So yeah, I took advantage of an opportunity. But I'm not the killer. If this company folds, I'll never get to be a star! Plus, I wouldn't want to hurt Anita even more. And she didn't kill him, either. Justin must have done it. He was jealous and he had access to the knife.

BEA: Yes, OK, obviously I realized my husband was having an affair with Holly. I'm sure it's not the first one either, the womanizer. But I didn't need to kill him! We were getting a divorce. I was going to have him out of my life anyway. I didn't have any reason to blackmail him either. I already had evidence he was cheating, and that was going to get me an excellent divorce settlement. And you know, I didn't even want him to die. We had a lot of good years together, and I suppose in some ways I still loved him. And I never went backstage, so I didn't have access to that prop knife. I bet that crazy Anita did him in.

HOLLY: I know what you all think, and that it looks bad, but I wasn't having an affair with Austin! I swear! I . . I did write that letter. I just can't explain it right now. I won't. That's my personal, private business. I'll just say that I cared about Austin very deeply and I would never have wanted any harm to come to him. And I can't imagine blackmailing or hurting anyone. I suppose it must have been Bea because she's jealous about what she thinks we did. I feel so responsible for that!

GUESS WHODUNNIT?

Give everyone five to ten minutes to discuss the clues and the statements. People can work alone, in couples, or in teams. Refreshments may be served at this point. Have answer slips ready so people can write down the name of the suspect they accuse, as well as their own name or team name. Collect the slips.

HEAR THE CONFESSIONS

Once all the answer slips have been collected, bring people's attention back for a second set of videos—this time, with each character admitting their secrets.

HOLLY: I guess there's no point in hiding it any more. Austin Jane is my father! He and my mother separated before I was born; he never knew about me. She put me up for adoption. She must have been very young. An agency was able to track down Austin for me. I'm glad we got at least a small chance to get to know each other. I wasn't having an affair with Austin and I'm not the killer.

ANITA: I have a secret as well. Twenty-five years ago, when we were high school sweethearts, Austin Jane got me pregnant. He left me before I could tell him. I gave the baby up for adoption, but my whole adult life I have wondered what happened to my daughter! That's why I knew that Austin and I would be together again—when I told him we had a child. I didn't know where she was, but I thought we could find her together. I'm no killer. And Holly! You're my daughter!

BEA: I'm happy you found each other, Anita and Holly. I truly am. And Holly, I'm so sorry I misunderstood what your meetings meant. I wish Austin would have told me. But our marriage was over anyway. I may have been wrong and jealous, but I'm not the killer.

JUSTIN: Holly . . . if you weren't having an affair with Austin . . . I was wondering if you'd like to go out sometime. I mean, maybe this isn't a good time to ask, right after a murder and all. But I thought I'd missed my chance once and I don't want to do it again! And you don't have to worry—I'm not the killer.

HUGH: Ugh. Everybody is just so disgustingly happy! Of course I knew about Holly all along. Do you think I'm an idiot? My sister went missing for nine months after a tryst with Austin years ago. Twenty-five years later, some perky ditz of exactly the right age shows up out of nowhere and starts having secret meetings with Austin? Hah. I put two and two together when I found that note about a secret meeting from Holly. She must be Anita's daughter! Well, I couldn't let the truth come out. It would kill her to find out who her daughter was that way! And she'd just get right back together with Austin, and then he could break her heart all over again! No way. And could I really let that jerk take my sister AND my starring role? Why does everything work out for him? I was more jealous than you realized, and I thought I was protecting my sister. I'm the killer!

WRAP-UP

People who got the correct answer will appreciate a chance to be recognized. During the final set of videos, a staff person can sort through the answer slips to find those that are correct. Put them in a bowl. After the killer is revealed, you can use the slips in this bowl to raffle off a few small prizes.

Further Reading

Karle, Elizabeth M. *Hosting a Library Mystery: A Programming Guide*. Chicago: American Library Association, 2009.

Kirby, Michael. How to Host a Murder Mystery . . . in Your Library. www .carleton.edu/campus/library/reference/workshops/MurderMystery.html.

chapter fourteen

Nerf Capture the Flag
Foam Dart Blaster Battle!

Community Need

Andrew Fuerste-Henry and Sarah Smith first heard about Nerf Capture the Flag as a program for kids. When they started their own monthly event for adults, they didn't have a proven community need in mind. They didn't know any adults who had Nerf guns or played this kind of game. But they did know one thing for sure: it sounded like a blast.

Once the program got going, the demand for social, physical play for adults quickly became clear. Within the first few months, the game developed a devoted core following. Those players brought their friends, and soon the events had a large and enthusiastic audience. Today, a few people even travel from out of state to play. Nerf gamers who had previously never set foot in the library now regularly attend programs and use library resources.

Source: Andrew Fuerste-Henry and Sarah F. Smith, Carnegie-Stout Public Library (IA)

While many of the programs in this book grew out of an established community need, there's still an important place for intuition and a sense of experimentation and fun. And after all, if you would love to go to an event, and your colleagues would love to go, and your friends—well, chances are you're not alone. Don't forget to make some space for your own sense of play!

PROGRAM LENGTH	PREPARATION TIME
2 hours	1 hour for set up and clean up

STAFF NEEDED

- 1–2 people (only 1 required for play; some libraries may prefer 2 for safety reasons)

MATERIALS

- 75 darts every other month
- 30 colored bandanas for team identification
- 1–2 spare blasters (Participants should bring their own.)
- Flags and bases. These don't have to be fancy—Andrew and Sarah made their flags from dowel rods and duct tape, and held them in bases made from traffic cones.

DIRECT COST

- Initial setup cost (bandanas, flags, bases): $100–$150
- Ongoing cost (darts): $20 every other month

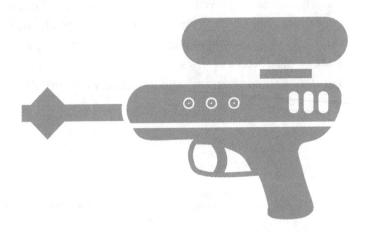

PROCESS

"We all know bookshelves are great for holding books, but did you know they're also very effective cover in a game of capture the flag?" asks the Carnegie-Stout Public Library's events calendar. Get ready for people to see your bookshelves—and your library—in a whole new way.

First, schedule this program after-hours, or on a day when the library is closed. It's going to be loud, messy, and fun!

Next, define the playing field. You can limit play to a specific (large) area of the library, with other spots out of bounds. For example, the reference desk, a second floor, or staff areas can be off-limits. Carnegie-Stout library also has a limited-play area—a mezzanine where each team is allowed to send a single "sniper."

On the field, place each team's flag in a spot that will be equally difficult to capture. Off the field, designate an area for players who are out or waiting their turn. Move tripping hazards or fragile items out of the way whenever possible, though you should ask players to be respectful and careful as well. Andrew has found it effective to remind his players that "if we break something or someone gets hurt, they'll never let us do this again."

Players arrive, bringing their own blasters (though it's not a bad idea to have a couple spares on hand at the library). Andrew and Sarah discovered that not only did many people already own blasters, they had customized them. Modifications that increase the range, power, or rate of fire are not allowed, but cosmetic upgrades are encouraged. Though players may bring their own unmodified darts, the library also supplies a communal pool. Any dart may be picked up and used by anyone during play.

Break the group into two opposing teams, and give each person a colored bandana indicating their team alliance. Each team begins with five players on the field; any additional players wait in the out-of-play area. Make sure all players are familiar with the rules and expectations before the game begins. Identify the staff person or volunteer serving as referee.

Start playing! Rounds last ten minutes each. Each team begins the round at their own base where their flag is held. A team scores one point when they have both flags (their own and the opposing team's) in their own base. When a team scores, someone from that team yells "Point!" The referee pauses the timer, verifies the score, and returns the flags to their starting locations. She waits at least thirty seconds for all players to return spent darts to the collective pot and go back to their bases before restarting play.

Of course, scoring points is just half the fun. Let's talk about blasters! Any person hit in the body (not the face or head and not on their blaster) by an opposing team member's dart is temporarily out. Holding their blaster above their head, they go to the designated out-of-play spot. There, they can tag in a waiting or previously shot team member. If someone is shot while carrying a flag, they drop the flag at the spot where they were tagged out.

In the last ninety seconds of the round, the referee announces "perma-death." At that point, any person shot remains out for the remainder of the round and no new players are tagged in. If all players on one team are eliminated, the opposing team scores a point.

Although this is a game with winners and losers, it is meant to be more fun than competitive. You will need to rely on the players to be honest and show good sportsmanship. Make sure that this is a clear expectation from the beginning, and be ready to work with the players to adjust the rules and play so that the game stays fair and fun for everyone.

Capture the Flag is just one possible game to play with blasters, and it may not be the right one for every library. It works best with a minimum of ten players in a space that is mostly symmetrical. If your space isn't ideal, your crowd is small, or you just have a group that wants to branch out, there are lots of other foam blaster games to try. Experiment with an all-out battle without the structure of the flags, try a last man standing death match, take inspiration from a first-person-shooter video game, or just make up your own!

Further Reading

Carnegie-Stout Public Library. Nerf Capture the Flag Rules. https://docs
.google.com/document/d/1NPQPkOiCAjfLIUOiVT9KfV9317
_3aBSJ-88-FEUbnT0/edit?pli=1.

Fuerste-Henry, Andrew, and Sarah F. Smith. "Why Should Kids Have All the
Fun?: Programs That Pop." (March 13, 2015). http://lj.libraryjournal
.com/2015/03/opinion/programs-that-pop/why-should-kids-have-all
-the-fun-programs-that-pop/#_.

chapter fifteen

Tabletop Gaming

A RECURRING SOCIAL gathering for modern board games.

Community Need

If the term "board game" instantly calls to mind your dusty childhood Parcheesi set, think again. Modern, engaging games for younger adults aren't just on a screen. A growing group of people are rediscovering the tactile, face-to-face fun of tabletop gaming. Game designers have been happy to oblige them with a wave of innovative, social, and highly sophisticated modern board and card games.

These real-world multiplayer games "engage [players'] imagination, spur critical thought . . . promote creativity . . . increase social engagement, and have the potential to be thought-provoking, challenging and, of course, fun," writes gaming guru John Pappas.[1] They encourage strategic and tactical thinking, storytelling, and interaction. Above all, they "build a culture of positive interaction" between people from different backgrounds and social groups.

Source: John Pappas, Bucks County Library System (PA)

Want to find the gaming community in your area? Start at what John has dubbed your FLGS—Friendly Local Game Store. You will meet local gamers, learn their favorite games, and get a sense of what kinds of events and environment they want. John's first gaming group at the Upper Darby Free Public Library grew out of visits to his FLGS. Some of the players he met were asking for more gaming groups than the store could provide, and others wanted a less intimidating environment for beginners. Spend some time there to find out what your local gamers need.

PROGRAM LENGTH	STAFF NEEDED	PREPARATION TIME
3 hours	1 person	½ hour to set up the space; more if you need to learn new games

MATERIALS

- 5–8 board and card games of varying difficulty and playing time
- 1 featured game
- 3–4 tables with chairs

DIRECT COST

- $30–$60 per feature game
- $10–$20 per short game

PROCESS

"[P]utting out a couple of games . . . and calling it a game night is like placing a pile of picture books and calling it a storytime," writes John.[2] A game night needs structure, variety, and facilitation in order to successfully engage a variety of people in a meaningful social and intellectual experience. While the games you select are important, the social arc of the night matters just as much.

Make this a recurring, regular event (weekly, monthly, or quarterly) from the beginning and plan to keep it consistent. An ongoing group has many opportunities for engagement and growth that a one-time event lacks. Aim for approximately ten people at your first event.

Set up several tables, each with a few games available to play. Choose games that are mostly familiar to the participants, whatever their level of experience. If your players are all beginners, include classic mass-market games like Clue or Scrabble. If they're more experienced, lean toward popular modern games like Settlers of Catan, Ticket to Ride, 7 Wonders, or King of Tokyo. It is helpful to have a variety of games and encourage attendees to reflect upon what made the games interesting, fun, and successful—this helps you develop a game menu that is tailored to your community.

Set up the featured game for the night on its own table. If you have a larger group with a few experienced players, you might even set up two copies on separate tables. Choose a game that accommodates three to eight people, can be played in an hour or less, and has simple rules. One person will teach and moderate this game, either a staff person or a regular participant sharing one of their favorites. Even if a volunteer teaches the game, you should make sure to be familiar with it.

However, you don't need to jump straight into the featured game. Instead, warm up the group with a short, easy game lasting ten to thirty minutes. These filler games help players relax, ease into the night of gaming, and get comfortable with each other. It also gives stragglers time to come in late without missing half the instructions for the featured game.

When it's time for the main game, the person running the program should moderate, not play. Explain the rules and help your participants along. When teaching a game for the first time, expect it to double the normal playing duration. Keep it fun, and make it safe for introverts to get engaged just as much as louder players.

When the featured game is over, disperse the players to other tables to choose their own games. People may decide to continue playing together in a large group, or to break up into smaller ones playing different games. When the evening starts winding down, facilitate one last quick, light game for everyone. This can be a simple card game (like Sushi Go!), a light dice game (like Zombie Dice), or a dexterity game (like Click Clack Lumberjack, Rhino Hero, or Jenga).

As participants learn new games each month, add the previously featured games to the additional tables so people can revisit their favorites. Also, once the players are familiar with the general mechanics used in modern board games, you can feature longer and more complex games. After a few months, encourage the group members to take ownership. Let them bring and teach their own favorites!

To make your first few meetings really successful, connect with your audience in advance. Use your FLGS, Facebook, Meetup, or other in-person and social media spaces where your local gamers are spending time. Are they beginners who want to start with familiar games, or experienced gamers who want to dive right in to more complicated ones? What kinds of games do they like? This connection is also crucial to letting your gaming community know that the event is happening. John notes that some of his groups had a large following from the first moments, while others took up to a year to develop a consistent group. Don't get discouraged.

With a little time and relationship-building, a game night has significant potential to grow and evolve. As it becomes more complex and participatory over time, it will bring a group of engaged, social learners back to your library again and again.

Further Reading

BoardGameGeek, LLC. Boardgamegeek. http://boardgamegeek.com.

Mayer, Brian, and Christopher Harris. *Libraries Got Game: Aligned Learning through Modern Board Games*. Chicago: ALA Editions, 2009.

Nicholson, Scott. *Everyone Plays at the Library: Creating Great Gaming Experiences for All Ages*. Medford, NJ: Information Today, 2010.

Pappas, John. "Board in the Library, Part One: An Introduction to Designer Board Games." *OCLC WebJunction* (December 30, 2013). www.webjunction.org/news/webjunction/board-in-the-library-part-one.html.

————. "Board in the Library, Part Six: Board Game Night Basics." *OCLC WebJunction*. (November 19, 2014). www.webjunction.org/news/webjunction/board-in-the-library-part-six.html.

Wheaton, Wil. Wil Wheaton's Tabletop. https://www.youtube.com/user/geekandsundry.

NOTES

1. John Pappas, "Board in the Library, Part One: An Introduction to Designer Board Games," *OCLC WebJunction* (December 30, 2013), www.webjunction.org/news/webjunction/board-in-the-library-part-one.html.

2. John Pappas, "Board in the Library, Part Six: Board Game Night Basics," *OCLC WebJunction* (November 19, 2014), www.webjunction.org/news/webjunction/board-in-the-library-part-six.html.

game menu for twenties to thirties

by John Pappas

These games are simple to learn, very social, and can play a large number of players—the perfect games to get a group playing, laughing, and enjoying board games in the library. These games may play a bit quicker than usual at twenty to thirty minutes, but they pack a big punch. Many of these games contain hidden roles and social deduction as their primary game mechanisms, and they create very social experiences for larger player counts.

1. **The Resistance: Avalon** (Hidden Roles, Social Deduction). Arthur and the knights represent the good of Camelot, yet hidden among them are Mordred's evil minions causing strife and distrust. The knights struggle to root out the minions before time runs out. The Resistance: Avalon plays five to ten people and plays in twenty to thirty minutes.

2. **Bang! The Dice Game** (Hidden Roles, Press Your Luck). It is the Wild, Wild West and you are either the sheriff, one of his deputies, an outlaw, or a renegade. Players roll dice to determine who they want to shoot, who they want to help, and whether the whole group will be ambushed. The goal is to pick off the people not on your team, but the whole game only lasts fifteen minutes so no one will hold much of a grudge.

3. **One Night Ultimate Werewolf** (Hidden Roles, Social Deduction). Players only have ten minutes to determine who the werewolves are from a group of villagers. At night everyone closes their eyes and each role wakes up in a certain order to apply their special ability. In the morning everyone deliberates to determine who is a werewolf. If the villagers find one werewolf and chase it out of town, the villagers win! If the werewolf remains hidden and an innocent villager is charged with lycanthropy, the werewolves win.

4. **Skull** (Bluffing). Skull is a game of pure bluffing. Each player is dealt four elegantly designed coasters consisting of one skull and three flowers. First player places one coaster facedown, and then each player in turn adds one more coaster. This goes on until someone feels confident enough that they place a bid on how many coasters they can turn over and reveal only flowers.

5. **Mascarade** (Hidden Roles, Social Deduction). Mascarade is a game that requires two specific skills: 1) being able to boldly lie to everyone at the table, and 2) being able to remember exactly who you are! At

the beginning of the game each player gets one of fourteen roles (King, Queen, Bishop, Inquisitor, Judge, Thief, etc.) each with its own ability. On a turn, players can either look at their card, declare themselves a role and take their action, or secretly switch with someone else. Be careful about calling out other players when they fib—are you even sure enough to know who you are?

6. **Ay, Dark Overlord!** (Storytelling). Players are either a group of goblin servants or the evil Dark Overlord. Basically, the dark plan has failed miserably and the Dark Overlord is not known to be forgiving. Each goblin has a hand of cards that allow them to craft elaborate excuses, pass the buck to other players, or interrupt the excuses of an active player. Don't panic, keep cool, and blame the heck out of the person next to you.

7. **Dixit** (Storytelling). Each player takes a turn as the storyteller and chooses one of the six images in their hand. They then make up a sound, lyric, song, poem, sentence, or general utterance that is related to the image. Players then bid on whose card is the storyteller's to earn points. The goal in this game is to be just clever enough that you confuse half the players but leave the others in the know.

8. **Citadels** (Card Drafting, Hidden Roles). In Citadels, players race to build their cities first. To do so they hire a character in each round to help them gain gold, erect buildings, and knock down their opponents. Then each player can earn gold or draw the plans for new buildings from the deck, and, if they can afford it, construct a new building.

9. **Incan Gold** (Press your Luck). In Incan Gold each player is an adventurer exploring an old temple in search of gold and treasure. However, there are several dangers ahead of the adventurers. The further you go, the more wealth you can gain, but if a hazard appears twice, you lose everything and run for the exit.

10. **Jungle Speed** (Dexterity). At the center of the table sits a wooden totem; each player is dealt a hand of cards. On each card there is a pattern and each pattern is nearly identical. Each turn, a player reveals a card. If it matches another player, they race to grab the totem. The winner of the race to the totem gives their discarded cards to the loser.

So that is it! With some shopping around you should be able to pick up all ten games for under $150. They will provide more than enough social gaming options to keep you knee-deep in the well of board games for at least a couple of years. You can always supplement them with some new classics like Ticket to Ride, Alhambra, or Carcassonne for those of us who are a little less socially inclined.

chapter sixteen

Story Night

SPEAK TRUTH TO laughter in a participatory evening of live storytelling.

Community Need

In Kitsap County, Story Night grew from a partnership. Local group StoryNight
.org was hosting a monthly live amateur storytelling event that attracted the
twentysomething- and thirtysomething audience the library hoped to reach.
Librarian Sarah Jaffa discovered the group as part of her efforts to get to know
the needs and interests of this target population. She approached its creator
and MC, Steve Gardner, to get to know more about each other's organizations.

Steve and Sarah quickly realized that a partnership would be of great benefit
to both. Story Night was already reaching the demographic we were targeting.
Partnering would help us connect with younger adults who love words and
stories—natural library users! Steve, in turn, wanted to grow the events, which
was difficult to do on his own. We provided PR to spread the word and staff

members to keep the events from being unsustainably dependent on a single person. Our Friends of the Library enriched the effort by donating small prizes and giveaways.

By working together, we doubled the regular attendance at Story Night. It is now consistently one of our most popular adult programs, often drawing fifty or more participants. Best of all, it is an incredible way to bring the library's mission of inspiration to the community. "Through shared effort, [we made] Story Night into something that celebrated the place of story in our lives, that fostered a sense of community and highlighted the talents of Kitsap County," Sarah says.

PROGRAM LENGTH	STAFF NEEDED	DIRECT COST
2 hours	1-2 people	$0–$25

PREPARATION TIME

- 1 hour for regular prep
- 2–3 if staff member is telling a story

MATERIALS

- Stage
- Microphone and speakers
- Small prizes

PROCESS

This event is based on the format used by the popular live storytelling series The Moth. It provides a forum for anyone to tell a story based on the evening's theme. The stories must be true, five minutes or less, and told without notes. "Just tell it like you were at a campfire," says Sarah. It's amazing to see the sense of community grow as people hear the best (or at least the bravest!) stories and storytellers from their own neighborhoods.

Set a theme for that night's stories; having a focus makes it easier for people to think of what to say. Keep it broad enough that many people will have a story on the topic. Examples from Kitsap's Story Night include Temporary Employment,

Outdoors, Advice, and Luck. Publicize the theme along with the event so that storytellers can think about what they'd like to say in advance.

Encourage storytellers to sign up ahead of time. They can let the library know a few days beforehand or sign up at the beginning of the session. Advance registration will give you a sense of how many storytellers you might have. If sign-ups are low, as they may be if your community doesn't know what to expect from an event like this, a staff member (or sacrificial friend or family member) may want to have a story prepared to fill possible gaps. When space remains, let last-minute storytellers add their names throughout the event.

On the night of the event, set up the space so that the audience can comfortably see and hear the speaker. Ideally, you will find a space with a permanent or portable stage and sound system. Kitsap Regional Library's group meets in a bar that has a stage and audio setup. If your library meeting room isn't ideal, think about local theaters or venues that might be good partners.

A dynamic MC will make the evening fun, smooth, and low stress. The Bremerton Story Night MC, Steve Gardner, begins by introducing the rules and the structure of the night. Storytellers will speak in a randomly selected order. If they approach the time limit, they will get a warning signal. This can be something as simple as holding up fingers for the remaining number of minutes. When everyone knows what to expect, the MC breaks the ice by telling his own short story on the night's theme.

After each story, the MC announces the next speaker and gives her a few moments to prepare. During that pause, he will pull a few short anecdotes from a hat. Audience members who are not telling stories are encouraged to toss in their own one to three sentence response to the theme for this purpose.

When all the stories have been told, the MC awards prizes. Three staff or audience members serve as judges and rate the stories with a point value. The story awarded the most points wins for that evening and is made available as a podcast. Winners and prizes are not necessary, but at Kitsap's events they seem to motivate people to come back the next month and try to win. If your audience is uncomfortable with competition, you can skip this aspect.

Prepare to be surprised by the variety and depth of the stories that are already in your community. In just one night you'll hear stories that are uproariously funny and terribly tragic, silly and serious, and just a slice of life.

Further Reading

Burns, Catherine. *The Moth: 50 True Stories*. London: Hyperion Books, 2013.
The Moth. http://themoth.org.
Story Night. www.storynight.org.

chapter seventeen

After-Hours Art Party
Night Light

LIGHT UP THE night with a monthly after-hours event of live art and delicious beverages.

Community Need

When Madison Public Library (WI) was ready to gut and renovate its Central Library, they threw a party. A really, really big party. For one day BOOKLESS turned the empty building over to DJs, artists, chefs, and anyone who wanted to come join in the fun. Five thousand people showed up.

Yes, five thousand.

"We realized, this is what the library should be like," says Trent Miller, who coordinates the Bubbler, the library's hands-on programming model. When the new library opened, they continued the spirit of after-hours, arts-infused, interactive adult play with Night Light. "It's 10 pm on a Friday, and there are 200 people in the library drinking beer and making screen prints," says Trent. "It's a really great way to bring people together."

Source: Trent Miller, Madison Public Library (WI)

That community building is the heart of Night Light's success. It fills a gap in the area for emerging adults who needed "something that wasn't a bar, where people could hang out and talk and do something creative, and be around other creative people that were interested in the same kind of thing," says Trent. "That's something that was kind of missing, and it felt like something we could do."

And they have. Night Light has fostered a community of its own, with adults coming together each month to celebrate and support creativity.

PROGRAM LENGTH	STAFF NEEDED
3 hours	1-2 people

PREPARATION TIME

- Varies based on the live event and artists

MATERIALS

- Varies based on the live event and artists. Common materials include:
    - Décor
    - Craft supplies
    - Catering

DIRECT COST

- $20–$500, depending on the event

PROCESS

On the first Friday night of each month the library throws a party featuring live performance and art. The live act might be music, dance, storytelling, performance art, or something a little less conventional: a grown-up pine derby race, an album launch, a camp night complete with ghost stories and merit badges. Every other month the library also debuts gallery shows from area artists. The festive environment is helped along by the cash bar provided by a local caterer.

Since community artists and organizations provide the acts and displays, the library's primary responsibility is coordinating the various people involved. MPL schedules the gallery shows for an entire year at one time. Artists apply for a slot in that year and a jury of library staff and local curators select the winning submissions. Live events, on the other hand, are planned four to five months in advance at the most. This leaves the schedule flexible enough to accommodate great ideas and opportunities that pop up. The art on display and the live event may or may not be directly related.

The coordination and communication needed to pull off a multifaceted event like this can be time-consuming. "Be flexible," advises Trent. "It's going to take more time than you think." However, allowing multiple simultaneous activities to cross-pollinate is a core part of this series' unique success. Each element attracts an audience that might not come without it. Together, they create an active, vibrant event that is "more rich, interesting, and weird" than any one piece alone.

Being strategic about staff involvement can make the coordination more manageable and successful. Because of the sense of community Night Light inspires, many of its attendees freely volunteer their time to help install art and prepare for the events. Yet, it is still important to have a main coordinator. This person should have a strong connection to the creative community the library hopes to reach. Trent's art background—he has an MFA in painting and has kept a foot in the local art scene—has been invaluable in facilitating relationships with partner artists and organizations. If your library does not have a staff member to fill this role, "hire towards that or find someone or a community group that wants to partner," advises Trent.

In contrast to the investment of time, Night Light can be done with minimal impact on the budget. The strong partnerships you build with local artists, performers, and businesses are really what support these events. Gallery artists are not compensated. Live performers may receive a small honorarium. The caterer sells directly to attendees without charging the library. Even with minimal funding your library can find its own local partners for some serious community-building revelry.

Further Reading

Bubbler. http://madisonbubbler.org.

Damon-Moore, Laura C., and Erinn Batykefer. *The Artist's Library: A Field Guide from the Library as Incubator Project.* Minneapolis: Coffee House Press, 2014.

Elias, Tana, and Janet Nelson. The Bubbler: An Innovative New Programming Model. December 4, 2013. http://ideas.demco.com/blog/bubbler-innovative-new-programming-model.

Library Journal. Trent Miller: Movers & Shakers 2015—Educators. 2015. http://lj.libraryjournal.com/2015/03/people/movers-shakers-2015/trent-miller-movers-shakers-2015-educators.

Madison Public Library. Bookless: Once in a Lifetime. 2012. www.urbanlibraries.org/bookless—once-in-a-lifetime-innovation-178.php?page_id=40.

Madison Public Library Foundation. Bubbler's Night Light Programming Helps Library Build Reputation as Popular Nightlife Venue. https://mplfoundation.org/news/view/bubblers-night-light-programming-helps-library-build-reputation-as-popular.

Ottosen, Sean, and Lucas Schneider. "Night Light at the Bubbler @ Madison Public Library." *Library as Incubator Project* (December 2, 2014). www.libraryasincubatorproject.org/?p=15674.

Spackle Madison. "Art Car Derby Takes Off with Flying Colors!" *Spackle Madison* (November 15, 2014). http://spacklemadison.com/art-car-derby-takes-off-with-flying-colors.

Thomas, Rob. "Quiet Riot: From Parties to Weddings to Hip-Hop Albums, Nobody Says 'Shhh' at the New Central Library." *The Cap Times* (November 26, 2014). http://host.madison.com/news/local/quiet-riot-from-parties-to-weddings-to-hip-hop-albums/article_edc2d2a1-d9b7-5e39-8ff3-a07ef179c371.html.

chapter eighteen

Library Speed Dating

FORGET COLLECTION MANAGEMENT—TRY love connection management. Bring singles in to the library for a night of speed dating.

Community Need

Talk about community building. Two couples are now married after meeting each other at Omaha Public Library's annual speed dating night. The original 2009 Hardbound to Heartbound event was one of the first of its kind in the United States. It won creators Manya Shorr and Amy Mather a spot among *Library Journal*'s 2010 Movers & Shakers. "OPL is all about connecting people with whatever they need to enrich their lives," says a library press release, "even if that means helping to find them a date!"

Source: Amy Mather, Omaha Public Library (NE)

The impact of speed dating events goes beyond helping a few young professionals find love. Programs like this demonstrate to a hard-to-reach population that the library is for them. "I want every single person to have an emotional connection to the library in the now, not its past," Amy said in her Mover & Shaker profile. "To succeed at this, we need to understand the patron's needs and fulfill them. . . . We cannot wait for patrons to tell us what they need. We need to go out and tell them how the libraries can help them."[1]

OPL holds this event annually on a weekend near Valentine's Day.

PROGRAM LENGTH	STAFF NEEDED	DIRECT COST
3-4 hours	6–10 people (1–3 staff members, plus volunteers)	$50–$500, depending on whether alcohol is sold

PREPARATION TIME

- 40 hours (10 prior to event, 30 after)
  - 10 hours to prep (2 a day to manage the wait list)

MATERIALS

- Décor
- Refreshments
- Score sheets

PROCESS

Dim the lights. Cue up some quiet music. Scatter chocolate kisses on your tables and set out pitchers of water. "Make it absolutely beautiful and comfortable," Amy advises. Your library is about to become the evening's best place to score a date.

When the night begins, don't be in a rush. Let people trickle in for the first fifteen to twenty minutes. The event will flow best if everyone is there before the speed dating starts. This time will also help people relax and get comfortable. For some, this will be their first speed dating experience. Give them a chance to find a drink or a snack and make their way to their seats.

Reserve one side of the tables for women, the other for men. When everyone is seated, let the dating begin! Each couple has three minutes to talk. The shy or tongue-tied can pick up one of the conversation starters scattered on slips of paper around the tables. OPL combines standards (Where did you go to high school? Vanilla or Chocolate?) with a few library-themed favorites (What's your favorite book? What type of music do you like?). Other libraries with similar programs ask people to bring a beloved book as their conversation starter.

At the end of the mini-date each person decides if he or she wants to meet their partner again. They privately record their date's name with a "yes" or "no" on their scorecard. Then the men move over one position while the women stay in the same spots. Have a few staff or volunteer wranglers on hand to help facilitate the transitions and avoid traffic jams. With new partners, the three minutes begin again.

With thirty men and thirty women in each age bracket (OPL offers age brackets for twenty-five to forty, thirty-five to forty-five, and forty-five+), the evening can get long. Don't feel obligated to keep people in their seats all night! Take a half-hour break in the middle. Let people stretch, refresh their drinks, and mingle casually for a while.

Currently, the OPL event is designed for opposite-gender couples. It initially included brackets for same-gender preferences, but OPL had to cancel this portion due to low registration. If your area has an LGBTQ community interested in speed dating be sure to include them from the beginning. For an example of a library that successfully combines straight and LGBTQ speed dating, check out Sacramento's alt+library program (*altlibrary.com*).

Throughout the night enjoy the loud, buzzy atmosphere. "Everybody's laughing and having a good time and having conversations," Amy describes. "It's always a full house—always wonderful." At the end of the evening, participants turn in their scorecards. In the following days librarians will contact pairs who both chose each other as a match.

The actual event is quick and easy to set up. Arrange tables and chairs for pair conversations, with clear movement pathways for the men to follow. OPL formerly used a single long table for each age group, but found the noise level and transition times to be a challenge. They are moving to a few shorter tables in the future. Set the mood with decorations and dim lighting. Designate a staff person to MC the event and ask a few other staffers or volunteers to help manage the crowd. The daters themselves will do the rest!

Be aware that speed dating requires significant staff time both before and after the dating experience. "It's a great event, it's pretty easy to put on, but there's a lot of management before and after," Amy admits. But she wouldn't give it up for the world. "It gets us so much publicity! It's a huge talking piece. That alone is worth doing it."

Prior to the event, the main task is managing registration. To be successful speed dating events need a critical mass of people—no fewer than fifteen of each gender per age bracket, but no more than thirty. Speed dating also needs even numbers of men and women in each group. Often the women's spots fill up almost immediately, while the men's registrations roll in over time. Compounding the complexity, this program is so hotly anticipated that some people try to sign up months in advance. OPL uses Eventbrite to help manage the flow.

To maintain this carefully curated balance it's important to minimize no-shows at the event. A week or so in advance, send out an e-mail blast to everyone registered. Remind them about the program and ask them to let you know if their plans have changed. Expect quite a few cancellations at this point and fill those slots with people from the waiting list.

But the real work comes after the evening ends. With 120+ participants, connecting the matches is a time-consuming challenge. OPL employees divvy up the work of identifying pairs who chose each other, recording each person's choices in a spreadsheet. This can take hours and is done over several days to a week after the event.

Once the matches have been identified, staff members send an e-mail that puts the parties in touch. For the risk management-minded, yes, it does contain a disclaimer. The bottom of the e-mail reads: "Please remember that participants in the Speed Dating event were not prescreened. Use caution when exchanging personal information, just as you would when meeting anyone for the first time. Omaha Public Library is free from any liability resulting from helping you make this connection." Sending these matches can take as much time or more as identifying them in the first place. But, of course, that's because so many people are finding potential partners at the library!

Even though this program takes a significant investment of staff time, its direct monetary costs are low and its impact is sky-high. "It's one of those surprises that people will always talk about," says Amy. OPL's event is still growing every year. "It's a great community connector. It's hard enough to go out and meet somebody . . . the library provides a safe and neutral space to make that connection." Years after its inception speed dating is still bringing new people into the library.

Further Reading

Wollan, Malia. "One Way to Encourage Checking-Out at the Library." *New York Times* (March 2, 2011). www.nytimes.com/2011/03/03/fashion/03dating.html?_r=0.

Zempleni, Flora. "Finding Love at the Library: A 3-Minute Speed-Date Chat Planted Seed of Romance for Omaha Couple." *Omaha.com* (February 26, 2015). www.omaha.com/news/metro/finding-love-at-the-library-a—minute-speed-date/article_3c93adc9–6f7c-5dc9–96eb-a666dad8646a.html.

NOTE

1. Omaha Public Library, Omaha Public Library Speed Dating Event Yields Another Love Connection (January 28, 2015), www.omahapubliclibrary.org/news-room/news-releases/1023—omaha-public-library-speed-dating-event-yields-another-love-connection.

CONCLUSION: EVALUATION

HOW DO YOU define success?

Answering this question is a crucial early step in planning any program. Evaluation should never be an afterthought, tacked on at the end of an event with some hastily printed surveys. (Admit it, you've done that.) Yes, evaluation can be surprisingly time-consuming, and on the surface it doesn't seem like the most fun part of program planning. But it makes a huge difference in how well you will be able to advocate for your playful adult programs, now and in the future.

In its simplest form, evaluation means knowing what success looks like and if you got there. *Getting Started with Evaluation* by Peter Hernon, Robert Dugan, and Joseph Matthews provides a concise overview of the steps that take you to that point: "identifying and collecting data about specific services or activities, establishing criteria by which their success can be measured, and determining the quality of the service or activity—the degree to which it accomplishes stated goals and objectives."[1]

Of course, you can only tell if you achieved your goals if you actually set them in the first place. The heart of evaluation is therefore setting goals at the beginning of your planning. What we normally think of as evaluation—checking to see how you measured up after the program—is just phase two. Patron surveys, attendance counts, and similar measurements cannot stand alone as evaluations. They are only meaningful if you know what goals your program was trying to achieve.

Just as evaluation doesn't begin with handing out patron surveys, it doesn't end there, either. Evaluation is meant to be used. Most of us are probably guilty of letting the occasional stack of surveys languish on our desks. But collecting data is not enough. The purpose of evaluation is to inform actions, to guide next steps. "Evaluation is a decision-making tool," we are reminded, "that is intended to assist library staff in allocating necessary resources to those activities and services that best enable the organization to accomplish its mission, goals, and objectives."[2] We need to analyze and draw lessons from the data we gather, or we have not really completed the evaluation process.

There are an almost endless number of ways to structure evaluations, and as many books, articles, and toolkits dedicated to them. Different strategies may work better for certain kinds of programs, or for certain libraries. Your organization may already have a framework in place. Therefore, instead of providing specific models that may or may not apply, this section will focus more generally on how to craft and use a powerful goal. That foundation remains meaningful regardless of the specific tool you choose.

Why Evaluate?

Well-designed evaluation creates an increasingly beneficial cycle that will improve the quality of your programs, help win the support of your coworkers and funders, and contribute to your own professional development. When you understand your program's goals from the very start, you have a clear guide for what elements are most important, and which can be eliminated or changed. The resulting program will be more intentional and focused than one created without goals in mind. In turn, that program will earn stronger buy-in from your organization and funders because you will be able to articulate why it matters and deserves support. When you complete your evaluation of that event, you can apply what you learned to the next one, starting you off with even better goals. The process begins again, improving every time.

We sometimes think of evaluation as a way to tell us when something is not working. But it's equally crucial to evaluate programs that are successful. Imagine that you try out a new idea for your system and it's a smash hit (of course!) How will you tell your manager, your board, and your local newspapers just how successful it was? You can't vastly exceed goals you never set. A framework for defining success will also help you connect your individual program's accomplishments back to the system's larger mission. How did you help people engage in lifelong learning? Who did you reach that wasn't previously coming to the library? What community needs did this program help address, and how well did it do that?

Or perhaps you take a leap into new territory, and the result is . . . okay. Attendance is middling, the PR wasn't effective, your budget was too small, or you struggled to find partners in the community. Do you continue the program or stop it? How long do you give it to improve and how do you know if that improvement is enough? Perhaps all it needs is a shift in the focus, venue, or timing, but how do you know what changes to make? You need to know where to invest your limited time, money, and energy. If you've started with a strong goal and assessed the program thoroughly, you will have the information you need to effectively answer these questions.

Learning from Failure

Sometimes, however, a program will be an outright flop. When trying something new we are all understandably a little haunted by the specter of possible failure. We may hesitate to set strong goals because we are afraid of the consequences of not reaching them. So let's talk about failure for a minute. Repeat after me:

Failure is good.

Really, failure is a good thing. That is not a playground-self-esteem cliché. Failing is a legitimate, important, and even necessary way to learn. The only way to avoid failing is to avoid taking risks. If you're not taking risks, you're not trying new things, not growing, experimenting, or learning. You're not reaching new users. You're not addressing evolving needs. Failure is a sign that you are thinking big.

The power of this mindset can be seen in start-up and entrepreneur culture. FailCon, "a conference for start-up founders to study their own and others' failures and prepare for success," meets all over the world (http://thefailcon .com). Founders@Fail (http://foundersatfail.com) is a community dedicated to learning from mistakes, with the motto "failure is fuel." Why are company founders—who often have significant investments on the line—so enamored with failure? Because they recognize that avoiding failure will hold them back from real success. "People's fear of failure restricts them from doing most of what they can do," warns venture capitalist Vinod Khosla.[3]

Successful CEOs and start-up founders regularly laud the value of failure in their own lives. "Fail fast and often," opines the CEO of VaynerMedia. "Failure is necessary and will happen if you are truly taking the risks required to make it."[4] Billionaire entrepreneur Mark Cuban agrees, saying, "I wouldn't be where I am now if I didn't fail . . . a lot."[5] Jonathan Long, founder and CEO of Market Domination Media, advises that "you have to embrace risk, and be willing to fail and fall flat on your face, sometimes several times, to reach your goals."[6] When you fail, realize that it's not the end of the path. If you learn from it, it's an important stepping stone to success.

Still feeling down after a failed program? Remember the main focus of this book—bringing back a spirit of learning through play. That's as true for us as it is for our patrons. In play, failure is not fatal. You lose a life, repeat a level, or sit out a round. But a few minutes later, you're right back in the game. The challenge increases your sense of triumph when you get it right and it teaches you how to get there. You are already building this attitude into your programs by encouraging adults to learn through nonjudgmental, experimental play. You can and should create them in the same spirit.

That said, in order to make failure a productive learning experience you absolutely must evaluate it.[7] What went wrong, by how much, and why? Was the issue with your overarching goal or its execution? Were there good parts of the program you could salvage and reuse? Who were they good for, and why? How do you know? Above all, what did you learn about your community's desires and needs? Dismissing your fear and negative emotions around failure allows you to ask yourself these questions clearly and objectively and learn from the answers. Evaluation can turn a misstep into the first step on a new journey.

How Do I Set Strong, Meaningful Goals?

First and foremost: plan for evaluation from the very beginning. Make it an integral part of your program's design. When you start with your goals you can engineer your project for success. Because you know what your priorities are and how you will measure them, every step is intentional and focused on achieving that goal. After the program, you will have the context to understand and make meaningful changes based on the data you gather. Integrated goals are naturally more meaningful than those added on after the program has been designed.

Of course, the better crafted your goal is, the more effective this process will be. A strong goal achieves many impacts: it guides your planning process; it makes clear why your program is important to the library and the community; and it gives you a yardstick to measure, report on, and learn from your experience. There are many, many frameworks and models that provide instruction on how to write a powerful goal. I will highlight a few common ones, not to endorse them over others, but because they are a simple way to illuminate general principles you can apply in any situation.

Get SMART

One way to evaluate the quality of a goal is to ask if it is SMART—specific, measurable, achievable, relevant, and time-bound. Even if you do not ultimately use the SMART framework or one of its many variants, the questions it prompts you to ask clarify some of the most important elements of a meaningful goal.

Note that the SMART acronym is used frequently in management literature, and as such has a variety of definitions and expansions. If you are interested in learning more, business and management literature is rich with detail and guidance.[8] The simple version I use in this chapter is the one I personally apply when setting goals in my library.

Is your goal specific? A *specific* goal is well defined, clearly identifying what you want to achieve. While that may seem obvious, this crucial first step is actually often implemented poorly. Because we don't want to fail, or because we don't set aside enough time for evaluation, it is tempting to avoid actually writing down a precise statement. But without a clearly stated goal, you won't be able to design the program to best meet it, won't know for certain if you have achieved it, and will probably struggle with figuring out how to measure it.

After specifying what you want to achieve, do you have a way to *measure* your results? How will you know if you're reached your goal or by how much you missed or exceeded it? And no, you cannot ever skip this step. The importance of measurement remains even if your goal is qualitative and hard to quantify. Even if the best measurable you can realistically track is not a perfect proxy for demonstrating achievement of your goal, it is one more piece of data that helps you make decisions and advocate for your programs. Do not make excuses to avoid measuring your outcomes. If you aren't measuring, you're depriving yourself of a key tool to advocate for your work.

At the same time, make sure the goal of your program is *achievable*. Do you actually have the time and resources to get this done? What would you need to give up or stop doing in order to make this happen? Goals should stretch and challenge you, but not push you past the breaking point. Even if you ultimately want a library packed full of twenty-seven-year-olds, if you've never gotten more than a handful at a program before, set a reachable goal this time. You can move the bar higher as your success grows.

Relevant gets relegated almost to the end of the acronym, but I wish it were first. Does your objective answer a community need or organizational priority? Your goal can be specific, measurable, achievable—and still be totally irrelevant to what your library and community care about. One of the great advantages of setting clear goals for your programs is that you can draw a direct connection to your organization's priorities. Your goal should clearly and explicitly relate to your library's mission, strategic plan, or annual goals. Usually, these will also reflect a need in the community. Your goal, and its attendant measurements, becomes a way of demonstrating exactly how much your programs are contributing to helping your library and community achieve their dreams.

Your goal should also be *time-bound*, meaning you know when the project is over. Does it have a concrete end date? If your program is a one-off with a self-evident ending point, make sure to time line out your planning. What steps need to be accomplished, when will they get done, and who is responsible for each one? Not only will this ensure that you have left yourself enough time to get things done, it will help you identify the support you need and communicate to your organization what goes into your programs.

Ongoing programs can also have time-bound goals. Before committing to something new indefinitely, consider it a pilot. Decide in advance at what point you will officially evaluate the project, and make a decision about whether or not (and how) to continue. Know at what intervals you will reevaluate long-standing programs to see if they are still meeting their goals and if those goals are still aligned with community and library needs.

When you set a goal that is specific, measurable, achievable, relevant, and time-bound, you ensure that your program is truly meaningful to you, your organization, and your community.

On the Outs

The SMART method gives you an idea of how to construct goals, but offers less guidance about the content of those goals. For that reason, I find it works best when partnered with an outcomes framework.

When libraries set goals they are often focused on inputs and outputs. Inputs are the raw materials we use for a program, like money and staff time. Outputs are the things we make and do. They may include how many programs we held, the number of people who came, how many books circulated this year, and how many visitors walked in our doors or used our computers. Libraries have been relying primarily on output measures to demonstrate our worth since the 1980s.[9] But outputs aren't truly meaningful to our communities and funders. They tell people what we do, but not why it matters or why they should care.

Outcomes, on the other hand, tell us "the real differences that the library makes in the lives of citizens."[10] They are the changes our work is affecting in the community. When people come to our programs, what do they learn that they didn't know before? What skills have they developed? How have their lives been improved? How has our library's mission been accomplished or a community need been addressed? Put simply, outputs are the what, and outcomes are the why.

The most powerful goals center on outcomes. Comparing a standard output-based goal to an outcome-based one reveals the strength of that difference. Perhaps you decide to put on Bad Art Night, one of the programs in this book. In the old output-based model, your goal might be to have twenty people attend. In the outcome-based model, your goal could be for adults to see themselves as more creative.

If you exceed your goal, in the first instance you will know that your program attracted twenty-two people. In the second, you will see that because of your program, participants now feel 22 percent more capable of creating and sharing art in their personal lives. The first is just a number, which without context is quickly forgotten. The second opens people's eyes to the importance of what we do.

Outcomes are qualitative and narratively powerful, but they still absolutely need to be measured. You're not off the hook! But you will need to apply a little more creativity because "determining how to measure outcomes can be a challenge."[11] The major appeal of outputs, and one reason we have relied on them so heavily, is that they are easy to measure. It is straightforward to track the number of people who attended your programs this year, and to report if that number went up or down. It is not so clear how to measure the ways those programs affected people's lives.

Therefore, outcomes need to be connected to measurements that can indicate their success. Some models call these Key Performance Indicators, or KPIs. Toolkits and guides that can help public libraries identify and collect the most meaningful measurements are beginning to appear, "but any library interested in improving its ability to demonstrate its effectiveness can begin the transition to becoming an outcome-oriented organization now."[12]

Think about what kinds of numbers would help demonstrate that your program achieved its goals. If the desired outcome is to create a more artistic community, the KPIs might include patrons' self-reporting on their creative confidence at the beginning and end of program, a follow-up survey response that they plan to or have created a piece of art on their own time since the program, or an increase in the circulation of art books or attendance at artistic programs. Now you are strategically analyzing those measurable inputs and outputs, not as stand-alone numbers, but as evidence that you achieved a higher outcome.

Imagine the difference this shift will make when you report on your programs to your manager, funders, and community. Instead of simply saying that a program was successful because twenty-two people attended, you can share that your program was successful because it contributed to creating a more vibrant, creative community. Then you can provide those outputs—attendance, survey results, etc.—as KPIs that demonstrate how and to what extent you are making your community a culturally richer place. Instead of talking about what you did, outcomes help you talk about the impact you had.

Outcome measurement is still fairly new in the world of public libraries. Because of that, one of the challenges of setting and measuring outcomes is the lack of precedent. There are not yet many published examples of outcomes for adults that other public libraries have set, or the indicators they used to measure them. However, guidance is not far away. Many academic librarians have embraced outcomes, and (thankfully!) researched and written about them. [13] Youth and after-school organizations have also successfully adopted outcome measures, and pioneering youth services librarians are now following suit.[14] Taking note of this trend, public library researchers and professional organizations have begun releasing toolkits, project results, and data for adult services.[15] As more librarians serving all age groups begin to think in terms of outcomes, selecting the most meaningful outcomes and KPIs will only become easier.

In the meantime, if setting SMART outcomes for your programs is a challenge, remember again to embrace a sense of play. It will not all be perfect the first time. Perhaps your goal turns out to be too ambitious or too easy, or your KPIs fail to align with your desired outcome as directly as you hoped they would. That's fine! Learn from that experience, and keep making adjustments and changes as you go. You don't have to get it all exactly right to start reaping the rewards. When you start seeing your programs as tools to strive for powerful shared goals, you will transform the way others see your work. Suddenly, your fun adult programs are not fluff or extras, but powerful community resources whose impact you can measure and prove.

Start with Evaluation—Start with Goals

Evaluation starts at the very beginning of any program idea. When you begin thinking about why you want to try a certain program, you are already formulating the goals that are the foundation of meaningful assessment. The most impactful goals will be specific, measurable, achievable, realistic, and time-bound (SMART), and will focus on outcomes (the difference we make in people's lives) rather than outputs (the stuff we make and do). Done right, evaluation is a powerful tool to guide your planning and advocacy, both before and after the program. It helps you learn from your successes and failures. And it focuses those around you on the deep, shared importance of what you do.

When you look at it that way, evaluation even starts to sound like fun.

NOTES

1. Peter Hernon, Robert E. Dugan, and Joseph R. Matthews, *Getting Started with Evaluation* (Chicago: ALA Editions, 2014).

2. Ibid.

3. John Boitnott, "Why Fear of Failure Is the Number One Thing Holding Back Entrepreneurs," *Inc.* (July 10, 2015), www.inc.com/john-boitnott/why-fear -of-failure-is-the-number-one-thing-holding-back-entrepreneurs.html.

4. Gary Vaynerchuk, "Gary Vaynerchuk: The Importance of Failure," *Inc.* (April 22, 2015), www.inc.com/gary-vaynerchuk/failing-is-absolutely-important.html.

5. Kim Lachance Shandrow, "Billionaire Entrepreneur Mark Cuban: 'Failure Is Part of the Success Equation,'" *Entrepreneur* (September 25, 2014), www.entrepreneur.com/article/237843.

6. Jonathan Long, "To Make It, You Have to Be Willing to Fall Flat on Your Face," *Entrepreneur* (August 25, 2014), www.entrepreneur.com/article/236737.

7. Gary Vaynerchuk, "Gary Vaynerchuk: The Importance of Failure," *Inc.* (April 22, 2015), www.inc.com/gary-vaynerchuk/failing-is-absolutely-important.html.

8. Good places to start include Project SMART (www.projectsmart.co.uk) and Arizona State University Professional Learning Library's online course *SMART Goals*, https://pll.asu.edu/p/content/smart-goals.

9. Joan C. Durrance, Karen E. Fisher, and Marian Bouch Hinton, *How Libraries and Librarians Help: A Guide to Identifying User-Centered Outcomes* (Chicago: American Library Association, 2005).

10. Ibid.

11. Meredith Schwartz, "Measuring Outcomes: Design4Impact," *Library Journal* (March 7, 2014), http://lj.libraryjournal.com/2014/03/opinion/design4impact/measuring-outcomes-design4impact/#_.

12. Carolyn A. Anthony, "Moving Toward Outcomes," *Public Libraries Online* (July 7, 2014), http://publiclibrariesonline.org/2014/07/moving-toward-outcomes/.

13. Denise Troll Covey, "Appendix D: Traditional Input, Output, and Outcome Measures," in *Usage and Usability Assessment: Library Practices and Concerns*, (Washington, DC: Council on Library and Information Resources, 2002), www.clir.org/pubs/reports/pub105/appendixd.html.

14. Deborah Vandell, *Afterschool Outcome Measures Online Toolbox*, 2015, http://afterschooloutcomes.org.

15. Examples include Public Library Association's *Project Outcome* (https://www.projectoutcome.org/), ALA's *National Impact of Library Public Programs Assessment* (http://nilppa.newknowledge.org), *Edge* led by the Urban Libraries Council (www.libraryedge.org), and the University of Washington iSchool's U.S. Impact Survey (https://impactsurvey.org).

FURTHER READING

Dudden, Rosalind F. *Using Benchmarking, Needs Assessment, Quality Improvement, Outcome Measurement, and Library Standards*. New York: Neal-Schuman Publishers, 2007.

Hernon, Peter, Robert E. Dugan, and Joseph R. Matthews. *Getting Started with Evaluation*. Chicago: ALA Editions, 2014.

Rubin, Rhea Joyce. *Demonstrating Results: Using Outcome Measurement in Your Library*. Chicago: American Library Association, 2006.

BIBLIOGRAPHY AND FURTHER RESOURCES

Alessio, Amy J., Katie LaMantia, and Emily Vinci. *A Year of Programs for Millennials and More*. Chicago: ALA Editions, 2015.

American Library Association. ALA Library Fact Sheet 17. 2014. www.ala.org/tools/libfactsheets/alalibraryfactsheet17.

———. National Impact of Library Public Programs Assessment. http://nilppa.newknowledge.org.

———. Rural, Native and Tribal Libraries of All Kinds Committee and American Library Association Office for Literacy and Outreach Services. *The Small but Powerful Guide to Winning Big Support for Your Rural Library*. Chicago: American Library Association, 2006.

Ansorge, Rick. "All Work and No Play Puts Adults Out of Touch: Playfulness Can Be Key to Creativity." *Colorado Springs Gazette—*Telegraph (December 21, 1990): D1.

Anthony, Carolyn A. "Moving Toward Outcomes." *Public Libraries* (May/June 2014): 5–7.

Arnett, Jeffrey Jensen. "Emerging Adulthood: A Theory of Development from the Late Teens through the Twenties." *American Psychologist* 55, no. 5 (2000): 469–80.

Arnett, Jeffrey Jensen, and Elizabeth Fishel. *When Will My Grown-up Kid Grow Up?: Loving and Understanding Your Emerging Adult*. New York: Workman Publishing, 2013.

Arnett, Jeffrey Jensen, and Jennifer Lynn Tanner. *Emerging Adults in America: Coming of Age in the 21st Century*. Washington, DC: American Psychological Association, 2006.

Barbakoff, Audrey. "Radical Home Economics: Programs That Pop." *Library Journal* (April 8, 2014). http://lj.libraryjournal.com/2014/04/opinion/programs-that-pop/radical-home-economics-programs-that-pop/#_.

_____. Words on the Water. September 2, 2012. http://boingboing.net/
    2012/09/20/words-on-the-water.html.

Boitnott, John. "Why Fear of Failure Is the Number One Thing Holding Back Entre-
    preneurs." *Inc.* (July 10, 2015). www.inc.com/john-boitnott/why-fear-of
    -failure-is-the-number-one-thing-holding-back-entrepreneurs.html.

Brickman, Sophie. "Recipe for a Better Book Club; When Cookbooks Are the Focus,
    the Benefits of Membership Are Tangible (and Tasty)." Wall Street Journal
    Online (May 24, 2013). www.wsj.com/articles/SB10001424127887324787004
    578495130943486190.

Brown, Alton. Hot Cocoa. www.foodnetwork.com/recipes/alton-brown/hot-cocoa
    -recipe.html.

Burns, Catherine. *The Moth: 50 True Stories.* 2013. London: Hyperion Books, 2013.

Carnegie-Stout Public Library. "Nerf Capture the Flag Rules." https://docs.google
    .com/document/d/1NPQPkOiCAjfLIUOiVT9KfV9317_3aBSJ-88-FEUbnT0/
    edit?pli=1.

Carruthers, P. "Human Creativity: Its Cognitive Basis, Its Evolution, and Its Con-
    nections with Childhood Pretence." *The British Journal for the Philosophy of
    Science* 53, no. 2 (2002): 225–49.

Coyne, Kelly, and Erik Knutzen. *Making It: Radical Home Ec for a Post-Consumer
    World.* Emmaus, PA: Rodale, 2010.

Damon-Moore, Laura C., and Erinn Batykefer. *The Artist's Library: A Field Guide
    from the Library as Incubator Project.* Minneapolis: Coffee House Press, 2014.

Davis, Paul M. "The Book Bike." *Shareable* (April 20, 2010). www.shareable.net/
    blog/the-book-bike.

Dillon-Malone, A. *Literary Trivia: Over 300 Curious Lists for Bookworms.* London:
    Prion, 2008.

Dossis, Nick. *Brilliant LED Projects: 20 Electronic Designs for Artists, Hobbyists, and
    Experimenters.* New York: McGraw-Hill, 2012.

Downtown Seattle Association. Transportation. 2014. www.downtownseattle.com/
    files/file/Transportation042914.pdf.

Dresser, Rocío. "Reviving Oral Reading Practices with English Learners by Integrat-
    ing Social-Emotional Learning." *Multicultural Education* 20, no. 1 (Fall 2012):
    45–50.

Dudden, Rosalind F. *Using Benchmarking, Needs Assessment, Quality Improvement,
    Outcome Measurement, and Library Standards.* New York: Neal-Schuman Pub-
    lishers, 2007.

Durrance, Joan C., Karen E. Fisher, and Marian Bouch Hinton. *How Libraries and
    Librarians Help: A Guide to Identifying User-Centered Outcomes.* Chicago: Ameri-
    can Library Association, 2005.

Elias, Tana, and Janet Nelson. The Bubbler: An Innovative New Programming Model. December 4, 2013. http://ideas.demco.com/blog/bubbler-innovative-new-programming-model.

Finch, Matt. "Dirty Library Trilogy, Part 1: Drink Your Way to Better Librarianship." The Signal in Transition (December 30, 2012). http://matthewfinch.me/2012/12/30/dirty-library-trilogy-part-1-drink-your-way-to-better-librarianship.

Francis, Chris. "Custom Library Book Bikes Roll Out Across US." *American Libraries* 45, no. 6 (June 2014): 18–19.

The Frugal Girls. Gifts in a Jar Recipes! http://thefrugalgirls.com/gifts-in-jars-recipes.

Fry, Richard A., and Jeffrey S. Passel. In Post-Recession Era, Young Adults Drive Continuing Rise in Multi-Generational Living. July 17, 2014. www.pewsocialtrends.org/2014/07/17/in-post-recession-era-young-adults-drive-continuing-rise-in-multi-generational-living.

Fuerste-Henry, Andrew, and Sarah F. Smith. "Why Should Kids Have All the Fun?: Programs That Pop." *Library Journal* (March 13, 2015). http://lj.libraryjournal.com/2015/03/opinion/programs-that-pop/why-should-kids-have-all-the-fun-programs-that-pop/#_.

G&R Publishing. *Gifts in a Jar: Cocoas, Cappuccinos, Coffees & Teas: Recipes to Make Your Own Gifts.* Waverly, IA: CQ Products, 2002.

Gabriel, Julie. *Green Beauty Recipes: Easy Homemade Recipes to Make Your Own Natural and Organic Skincare, Hair Care, and Body Care Products.* Royal Tunbridge Wells, UK: Petite Marie Ltd., 2010.

Gella. Let It Glow Holiday Cards. https://learn.sparkfun.com/tutorials/let-it-glow-holiday-cards.

Get Involved: Powered By Your Library. From Book to Action: One Library's Story. 2012. https://www.youtube.com/watch?v=tOkDOYR5Pb4.

Gorman, Michael. *Our Enduring Values: Librarianship in the 21st Century.* Chicago: American Library Association, 2000.

———. *Our Enduring Values Revisited: Librarianship in an Ever-Changing World.* Chicago: ALA Editions, 2015.

Gregerman, Alan S. *Lessons from the Sandbox: Using the 13 Gifts of Childhood to Rediscover the Keys to Business Success.* Lincolnwood, IL: Contemporary Books, 2000.

Gross, Valerie J. "Transforming Our Image through Words That Work: Perception in Everything" *Public Libraries* (Sep/Oct 2009): 24–32.

Hernon, Peter, Robert E. Dugan, and Joseph R. Matthews. *Getting Started with Evaluation.* Chicago: ALA Editions, 2014.

Hirsh-Pasek, Kathy, Roberta M. Golinkoff, and Diane E. Eyer. *Einstein Never Used Flash Cards: How Our Children REALLY Learn—and Why They Need to Play More and Memorize Less.* Emmaus, PA: Rodale, 2003.

Institute of Museum and Library Services. *Growing Young Minds: How Museums and Libraries Create Lifelong Learners.* United States: Institute of Museum and Library Services, 2013. www.imls.gov/assets/1/AssetManager/GrowingYoungMinds.pdf.

_____. *Public Libraries in the United States Survey: Fiscal Year 2011.* Washington, DC: Institute of Museum and Library Services, 2014.

Instructables. Making an Electro Card Using Bare Paint! http://makeitatyourlibrary.org/technology/making-electro-card-using-bare-paint#.VbhPb7dcRpn.

Johnson, Lizzie. "Spoke & Word Bike Takes S.F. Library to the Streets." *San Francisco Chronicle* (July 24, 2015). www.sfchronicle.com/bayarea/article/Spoke-Word-bike-takes-S-F-library-to-the-6404867.php.

Jones, Jeffrey M. In U.S., 14% of Those Aged 24 to 34 Are Living with Parents. February 13, 2014. www.gallup.com/poll/167426/aged-living-parents.aspx.

Karle, Elizabeth M. *Hosting a Library Mystery: A Programming Guide.* Chicago: American Library Association, 2009.

Kirby, Michael. How to Host a Murder Mystery . . . in Your Library. www.carleton.edu/campus/library/reference/workshops/MurderMystery.html.

Lear, Brett W. *Adult Programs in the Library, Second Edition.* Chicago: ALA Editions, 2013.*Library Journal.* Cooking Reviews. http://reviews.libraryjournal.com/category/books/nonfic/sci-tech/.

Library Journal. Trent Miller: Movers & Shakers 2015—Educators. 2015. http://lj.libraryjournal.com/2015/03/people/movers-shakers-2015/trent-miller-movers-shakers-2015-educators.

Long, Jonathan. "To Make It, You Have to Be Willing to Fall Flat on Your Face." *Entrepreneur* (August 25, 2014). www.entrepreneur.com/article/236737.

Lowe's Creative Ideas. Make Hypertufa Pots. www.lowes.com/creative-ideas/woodworking-and-crafts/make-hypertufa-pots/project.

Madison Public Library. Bookless: Once in a Lifetime. 2012. www.urbanlibraries.org/bookless—once-in-a-lifetime-innovation-178.php?page_id=40.

Madison Public Library Foundation. Bubbler's Night Light Programming Helps Library Build Reputation as Popular Nightlife Venue. https://mplfoundation.org/news/view/bubblers-night-light-programming-helps-library-build-reputation-as-popular.

The Martha Stewart Show. Hypertufa Pots. 2010. www.marthastewart.com/268962/hypertufa-pots.

Mayer, Brian, and Christopher Harris. *Libraries Got Game: Aligned Learning through Modern Board Games.* Chicago: American Library Association, 2010.

McGonigal, Jane. *Reality Is Broken: Why Games Make Us Better and How They Can Change the World.* New York: Penguin Press, 2011.

Molaro, Anthony, and Leah L. White. *The Library Innovation Toolkit: Ideas, Strategies, and Programs.* Chicago: ALA Editions, 2015.

Moore, Ian. "Sacramento Library Inspires Bad Artists." *Sacramento Press* (December 17, 2010). http://sacramentopress.com/2010/12/17/sacramento-library -inspires-bad-artists/.

National Science Foundation. Enough with the Lecturing. May 12, 2014. https:// www.nsf.gov/news/news_summ.jsp?cntn_id=131403.

New York Public Library. "NYPL Now!" 2014. www.nypl.org/events/now-online.

Nicholson, Scott. *Everyone Plays at the Library: Creating Great Gaming Experiences for All Ages.* Medford, NJ: Information Today, 2010.

————. "Games in Libraries: Myths and Realities." *NYLA Bulletin* 56, no. 4 (2008): 3.

————. "A Recipe for Meaningful Gamification." In *Gamification in Education and Business.* Wood, L., and Reiners, T., eds. Switzerland: Springer, 2015.

————. "Strategies for Meaningful Gamification: Concepts Behind Transformative Play and Participatory Museums." Lansing, MI: Paper presented at *Meaningful Play,* 2012.

Nwoye, Irene Chidinma. "Meet the Two New Yorkers Who Are Starting a Preschool for Adults." *The Village Voice* (January 30, 2015). www.villagevoice.com/news/ meet-the-two-new-yorkers-who-are-starting-a-preschool-for-adults-6686092.

Oldenburg, Don. "Learning from the Minds of Babes; Book Brings Sandbox Creativity to Workplace." *The Washington Post* (September 14, 2000): C.4.

Oldenburg, Ray. *The Great Good Place: Cafés, Coffee Shops, Bookstores, Bars, Hair Salons, and Other Hangouts at the Heart of a Community.* New York: Marlowe, 1999.

Ottosen, Sean, and Lucas Schneider. "Night Light at the Bubbler @ Madison Public Library." *Library as Incubator Project* (December 2, 2014). www.library asincubatorproject.org/?p=15674.

Palmer, Alex. *Literary Miscellany: Everything You Always Wanted to Know About Literature.* New York: Skyhorse Publishing, 2010.

Pappas, John. "Board in the Library, Part One: An Introduction to Designer Board Games." *OCLC WebJunction* (December 30, 2013). www.webjunction.org/ news/webjunction/board-in-the-library-part-one.html.

————. "Games in Libraries: Myths and Realities." *NYLA Bulletin* 56, no. 4 (2008): 3.

"Board in the Library, Part Six: Board Game Night Basics." *OCLC WebJunction* (November 19, 2014). www.webjunction.org/news/webjunction/board-in-the -library-part-six.html.

Penenberg, Adam L. *Play at Work: How Games Inspire Breakthrough Thinking.* New York: Portfolio Hardcover, 2013.

Perelman, Deb. Decadent Hot Chocolate Mix. December 4, 2014. http://smitten kitchen.com/blog/2014/12/decadent-hot-chocolate-mix/.

Philanthropy News Digest. "More Millennials Value Volunteering Than Previous Generation Did." *Philanthropy News Digest* (January 5, 2015). http:// philanthropynewsdigest.org/news/more-millennials-value-volunteering -than-previous-generation-did.

Pigza, Jessica. *BiblioCraft: The Modern Crafter's Guide to Using Library Resources to Jumpstart Creative Projects.* New York: STC Craft, 2014.

Putnam, Robert D. *Bowling Alone: The Collapse and Revival of American Community.* New York: Simon & Schuster, 2000.

Rapinchuk, Becky. *The Organically Clean Home: 150 Everyday Organic Cleaning Products You Can Make Yourself—the Natural, Chemical-Free Way.* Avon, MA: Adams Media, 2014.

Rubin, Rhea Joyce. *Demonstrating Results: Using Outcome Measurement in Your Library.* Chicago: American Library Association, 2006.

Russ, Sandra Walker. *Pretend Play in Childhood: Foundation of Adult Creativity.* Washington, DC: American Psychological Association, 2014.

Sacramento Public Library. Alt+Library Bad Art Night. http://altlibrary.com/tag/ bad-art-night/.

_____. Alt+Library Book Club. http://altlibrary.com/altlibrary-book-clubs-2/.

San Francisco Public Library. "S.F. Public Library Rolls out New Book Bike Named Spoke & Word." April 17, 2015. http://sfpl.org/releases/2015/04/17/s-f -public-library-rolls-out-new-book-bike-named-spoke-word/.

Schwartz, Meredith. "Measuring Outcomes: Design4impact." *Library Journal* (March 7, 2014). http://lj.libraryjournal.com/2014/03/opinion/design4impact/ measuring-outcomes-design4impact/#_.

Shandrow, Kim Lachance. "Billionaire Entrepreneur Mark Cuban: 'Failure Is Part of the Success Equation.'" *Entrepreneur* (September 25, 2014). www.entrepreneur .com/article/237843.

Shank, Jenny. "Bright Orange 'Book Bikes' Signify Changing Times for Libraries." *MediaShift* (September 24, 2014). http://mediashift.org/2014/09/bright -orange-book-bikes-signify-changing-times-for-libraries/.

Siegel-Maier, Karyn. *The Naturally Clean Home: 150 Super-Easy Herbal Formulas for Green Cleaning.* North Adams, MA: Storey Publishing, 2008.

Spackle Madison. "Art Car Derby Takes Off with Flying Colors!" *Spackle Madison* (November 15, 2014). http://spacklemadison.com/art-car-derby-takes-off -with-flying-colors.

Stewart, Martha. Homemade Hot Chocolate. www.marthastewart.com/353001/ homemade-hot-chocolate.

Szuecs, Joe. "Hypertufa Planter: Maximum Zen for Minimum Yen." *Make: Projects.* http://makezine.com/projects/hypertufa-planter/.

Tanner, Jennifer Lynn. "Recentering During Emerging Adulthood: A Critical Turning Point in Life Span Human Development." In *Emerging Adults in America: Coming of Age in the 21st Century*, edited by Jeffrey Jensen Arnett. Washington, DC: American Psychological Association, 2006.

Thomas, Rob. "Quiet Riot: From Parties to Weddings to Hip-Hop Albums, Nobody Says 'Shhh' at the New Central Library." *The Cap Times* (November 26, 2014). http://host.madison.com/news/local/quiet-riot-from-parties-to-weddings-to-hip-hop-albums/article_edc2d2a1-d9b7-5e39-8ff3-a07ef179c371.html.

Thomas, Sally. *Book-to-Action Toolkit.* California: California State Library, 2012. www.library.ca.gov/lds/getinvolved/booktoaction/docs/Final-Toolkit-large.pdf.

University of Washington Information School, U.S. Impact Study, and Bill and Melinda Gates Foundation. *Impact Survey.* https://impactsurvey.org.

Vandell, Deborah. *Afterschool Outcome Measures Online Toolbox.* 2015. http://afterschooloutcomes.org.

Vaughn, Susan. "Zen at Work; To Think Outside Box, Get Back Into Sandbox; Now That Creativity Can Mean Corporate Survival, Employees Have to Learn How to Make Work into Child's Play." *Los Angeles Times* (January 11, 1999): 3.

Vaynerchuk, Gary. "Gary Vaynerchuk: The Importance of Failure." *Inc.* (April 22, 2015). www.inc.com/gary-vaynerchuk/failing-is-absolutely-important.html.

Velden, Dana. "Good Idea: Start a Food Lit or Cookbook Book Club." *The Kitchn* (February 8, 2010). www.thekitchn.com/good-idea-start-a-food-lit-or-108115.

White, Leah. "Books on Tap: The Book Group That Meets in a Bar." *Marketing Library Services* 27, no. 5 (2013). www.infotoday.com/mls/sep13/White—Books-on-Tap—The-Book-Group-That-Meets-in-a-Bar.shtml.

———. "The Modern Book Club (Meets in a Bar)." *Letters to a Young Librarian* (2013). http://letterstoayounglibrarian.blogspot.com/2013/01/the-modern-book-club-meets-in-bar-by.html.

Wolfer, Alexis, and Evan Sung. *The Recipe for Radiance: Discover Beauty's Best-Kept Secrets in Your Kitchen.* Philadelphia, PA: Running Press, 2014.

Wollan, Malia. "One Way to Encourage Checking-Out at the Library." *New York Times* (March 2, 2011). www.nytimes.com/2011/03/03/fashion/03dating.html?_r=0.

Zempleni, Flora. "Finding Love at the Library: A 3-Minute Speed-Date Chat Planted Seed of Romance for Omaha Couple." *Omaha.com* (February 26, 2015). www.omaha.com/news/metro/finding-love-at-the-library-a—minute-speed-date/article_3c93adc9-6f7c-5dc9-96eb-a666dad8646a.html.

Zickuhr, Kathryn, and Lee Rainie. Younger Americans and Public Libraries: How Those under 30 Engage with Libraries and Think about Libraries' Role in Their Lives and Communities. Washington, DC: Pew Research Center, 2014. www.pewinternet.org/files/2014/09/PI_YoungerAmericansandLibraries_091014.pdf.

Zickuhr, Kathryn, Kristen Purcell, and Lee Rainie. From Distant Admirers to Library Lovers—and Beyond: A Typology of Public Library Engagement in America. Washington, DC: Pew Research Center, 2014. www.pewinternet.org/files/2014/03/PIP-Library-Typology-Report.pdf.

Zickuhr, Kathryn, Lee Rainie, and Kristen Purcell. Younger Americans' Library Habits and Expectations. Washington, DC: Pew Research Center, 2014. http://libraries.pewinternet.org/files/2013/06/PIP_Younger_Americans_and_libraries.pdf.

Further Resources

The programs listed in this book are just a few of the endless possibilities for incorporating adult play into your library. Resources to help you delve deeper into the themes of each program are listed at the end of the event descriptions. When you want to explore more ideas than you find in these pages, turn to one of these adult programming resources for inspiration.

Alessio, Amy J., Katie LaMantia, and Emily Vinci. *A Year of Programs for Millennials and More*. Chicago: ALA Editions, 2015.

American Library Association Public Programs Office. Programming Librarian. http://programminglibrarian.org.

Damon-Moore, Laura C., and Erinn Batykefer. *The Artist's Library: A Field Guide*. Minneapolis: Coffee House Press, 2014.

Lear, Brett W. *Adult Programs in the Library, Second Edition*. Chicago: ALA Editions, 2013.

Library as Incubator Project. (www.libraryasincubatorproject.org).

Make It @ Your Library. (http://makeitatyourlibrary.org).

McGonigal, Jane. *Reality Is Broken: Why Games Make Us Better and How They Can Change the World*. New York: Penguin Press, 2011.

Molaro, Anthony, and Leah L. White. *The Library Innovation Toolkit: Ideas, Strategies, and Programs*. Chicago: ALA Editions, 2015.

Nicholson, Scott. *Everyone Plays at the Library: Creating Great Gaming Experiences for All Ages*. Medford, NJ: Information Today, 2010.

Pigza, Jessica. *BiblioCraft: The Modern Crafter's Guide to Using Library Resources to Jumpstart Creative Projects*. New York: STC Craft, 2014.

Pinterest. (https://www.pinterest.com).

ABOUT THE AUTHOR AND CONTRIBUTORS

AUDREY BARBAKOFF is the adult services manager at Kitsap Regional Library in Washington State. For her innovative adult programming, she was named a 2013 *Library Journal* Mover & Shaker and one of Flavorwire's "10 of the Coolest Librarians Alive." She speaks and writes extensively on revitalizing adult programming, with a focus on emerging adults. Her articles have appeared in *Library Journal*, *Strategic Library*, and *The Library Innovation Toolkit*, and she has presented at ALA, the Washington Library Association conference, and in various webinars.

CHRISTY ESTROVITZ is the manager of youth services for the San Francisco Public Library in San Francisco, California, known for building vibrant partnerships, innovative programs, and event planning for all ages. She is the go-to-gal for the Spoke & Word, the library's book bike.

ANDREW FUERSTE-HENRY is the adult services manager at Carnegie-Stout Public Library in Dubuque, Iowa. He is the ALA Chapter Councilor for Iowa and has written and presented on collection development for graphic novels. He favors the Nerf CycloneShock for reliability and ease of reloading, but sometimes switches to the Demolisher 2-in-1 for increased dart capacity.

TRACY GOSSAGE is a reader services librarian at Northbrook Public Library in Illinois. In addition to facilitating Books on Tap, she is involved in implementing a variety of adult programming, creating content for the library's social media presence, and providing front-line readers' advisory in a fun and courteous manner.

SARAH JAFFA is an adult services librarian at Kitsap Regional Library in Washington State. She specializes in collection development and community engagement through programming and outreach. She serves on the RUSA/CODES Notable Book Council and leads the Kitsap Regional Library Readers Advisory team.

AMY MATHER serves as the adult services manager for Omaha Public Library in Nebraska. Outreach initiatives include Omaha Reads, downtown Omaha lit fest, Read It & Eat: A Culinary Conference, and a yearly Speed Dating event. As part of her outreach initiatives, she was recognized along with a colleague as one of *Library Journal*'s Movers & Shakers in 2010. She currently serves on daOMA (design alliance Omaha) board, graduated from Leadership Omaha, a ten-month program to develop community leaders, and was recognized for her Whatever Mathers podcast conversation with Omaha creatives, in the *B2B Omaha Magazine*.

TRENT MILLER is an artist, curator, and the head Bubblerarian at Madison Public Library in Madison, Wisconsin, where he is spearheading the library's makers'-focused program called The Bubbler. He was recently recognized by *Library Journal* as a 2015 Mover & Shaker. Miller centers his energies on establishing the public library as a platform for creative and innovative art events, shows, and workshops, with an emphasis on local creators.

JOHN PAPPAS is a library manager at the Bucks County Library System in Bensalem, Pennsylvania. Prior to that, he was the outreach and programming coordinator at the Rapid City Public Library System in Rapid City, South Dakota. He is the author of the "Board in the Library" series on Webjunction, co-presenter of the webinar, "The Golden Age of Gaming: Board Games for Grown-Ups," as well as the editor of the blog, boardinthelibrary.com, which focuses on the intersection of gaming and libraries. He is a member-at-large in ALA's GameRT (Games and Gaming Round Table) and has spoken at several local and national conferences on adult programming, board game design and development, successful gamification, and circulating board game collections. He is currently developing three books on using board games to help teach social and job readiness skills and ethics.

SARAH SMITH is an adult services librarian at Carnegie-Stout Public Library in Dubuque, Iowa. She is the president of the Readers' Advisory Roundtable of the Iowa Library Association and has presented workshops at regional conferences on providing readers' advisory services to adults. When she isn't shooting people with Nerf blasters or talking about books, you'll find her devising ways to build sonic screwdrivers for under $5 or creating custom fabric stencils.

JESSICA ZAKER is the central branch manager for the Sacramento Public Library in Sacramento, California, and head coach of the Sac City Rollers roller derby league. She has been offering alternative programming in Sacramento for the last seven years and is lucky enough to have a roller skate commute.

INDEX